James Felkey

What Everyone Needs to Know About Law

What Everyone Needs to Know About Law

BOOKS by U.S.NEWS & WORLD REPORT

Joseph Newman—Directing Editor

A division of U.S.News & World Report, Inc.

WASHINGTON, D.C.

2300 N. Street N.W., Washington, D.C. 20037

Library of Congress Catalog Card Number 79-156271

Printed in the United States of America

Contents

Acknowledgments

In preparing the manuscript for *What Everyone Needs to Know About Law*, the editors of the Book Division of U.S.News & World Report, Inc., have had the benefit of the knowledge and experience of a number of lawyers and legal authorities. For his assistance in helping to collect this large body of material and to clarify its meaning, a special word of recognition is due to Merle F. Wilberding, a member of the bars of the District of Columbia and the State of Iowa. For reading the manuscript in advance of publication, thanks are due to Professor Herbert Peterfreund, of the New York University School of Law, and to Professor Edward J. Murphy, of the Notre Dame Law School. Miss Linda Glisson, a member of the staff of the Book Division, served as editorial coordinator for this book.

Chapter One

An Introduction to Law

Every day of our lives, we are restrained and guided by law. It protects us while it restricts us. Sometimes it punishes us. In subtle ways, a complex and voluminous set of laws governs our every action. It determines the registration of our births and the distribution of our possessions at death. It tells us how fast we can drive and how long we must attend school. Through zoning laws, it restricts the type of home we build. Through gambling and drinking laws, it regulates the life we lead. Through the Federal Communications Commission, it determines the entertainment we see on TV. Through the Federal Trade Commission, it helps to protect us from unfair commercial practices. There is no end to the ways in which the law significantly affects our lives.

The scope of the law necessarily makes it complex, and complexity has created the need for specialists, namely lawyers. This puts the practice of law well beyond the reach of the layman, and this book does not propose to perform the magic of turning laymen into lawyers. Such undertakings invariably mislead the reader and cause trouble. For legal assistance in specific instances, the services of a competent professional usually is advisable.

However, the fact that the law touches us so closely and

so frequently makes it also advisable that the layman have a general understanding of its character. This book hopes to promote such an understanding, particularly in those areas which bear most closely on our daily lives. At the same time, it may prepare the reader for a better informed and more satisfactory relationship with his lawyers—and the courts, should such an encounter become necessary.

Basically, law is a system of rules. Members of a society establish these rules in order to live in relative harmony. To achieve this end, the individual relinquishes certain rights for the good of the group. For example, each person in this country has surrendered the right to drive on the left side of the highway in order for everyone to drive in relative safety.

Law can also be defined as a standard of conduct which regulates the relation of the individual to the central government, the relation of the government to the individual, and the relations among individuals. If there is a conflict in these relations, the law also provides an institution, the court system, through which the respective sides can litigate a problem and reach a solution.

The court is used to determine conflicts between two individuals and to provide a forum for the enforcement of criminal law. The United States possesses a unique court system in that there is a state system and a federal system.

State courts determine almost all questions concerning wills, crime, contracts, personal injuries, and domestic relations. Federal jurisdiction is invoked in questions concerning the United States Constitution, federal laws, conflicts between states, and civil suits involving citizens of different states. This last category is called diversity jurisdiction. Although cases involving federal statutes are usually heard in federal courts, some can be heard in state courts as well.

In general, state courts hear both civil and criminal cases. Jurisdiction in the two areas of law is often established by separate statutes. Usually, at any one time, some judges are assigned to criminal cases while others hear civil cases. However, the method of assigning cases varies among the different states.

In a civil case, a dispute between individuals is heard and determined. If the individuals desire, they usually can have the case heard before a jury selected from the community. However, some states do not provide jury trials for all civil actions. Thus, if the individual wishes or the state requires it, a judge will hear the case alone. An example of a civil suit would be as follows: Baker sues Dodd for damages resulting from injuries sustained in an automobile accident. This is a case between individuals, not between the state and an individual.

In a state criminal court, the judge and jury determine whether the state has proven its criminal charges beyond a reasonable doubt. If the state fails to prove its case, the defendant will be acquitted. If the jury is satisfied beyond a reasonable doubt that the defendant is guilty, it will convict him. However, it should be noted that a criminal defendant also can waive his right to a jury trial and appear solely before a judge.

Essentially, the federal court was established to decide the law in cases concerning the Constitution, federal laws, citizens of diverse states, and conflicts between states. In the first situation the court is asked to apply a specific constitutional provision or to settle a case arising out of a federal statute, either civil or criminal. In other words, it decides a "federal question." Secondly, the court settles private disputes between two individuals who are citizens of different states. In this situation, it might be unfair to force one litigant into the state court system of the other. Therefore, the federal court system may handle these diversity suits. However, they can be heard in a state court if that court obtains jurisdiction over both parties.

Both the state and federal court systems have courts of original jurisdiction and courts of appellate jurisdiction. The court of original jurisdiction is also known as the trial court. It is in this court that a civil or criminal proceeding is started and initially decided. A civil proceeding, for example, begins when the plaintiff files his complaint with the court. This is a legal document in which the plaintiff alleges that another person has injured him in some way and requests damages or other relief for the injury. When the judge or jury brings in a verdict, the initial civil or criminal proceeding is complete.

What happens if the loser of the trial believes that certain substantive or procedural laws were violated during the proceeding? He can appeal the case to a court of appellate jurisdiction. Both the state and federal court systems have appellate courts. A court of appellate jurisdiction reviews the proceedings at the trial level and determines whether the trial court's decision should be affirmed or reversed. In general, if the litigant files an appeal, the appellate court must consider the case and render its opinion.

There are several tiers of appellate courts. Consequently, if one court rules against him, the litigant often is able to appeal his case to a higher appellate court. However, some state court systems have only one appellate court above the trial court. Decisions of both federal and state courts can be reviewed by the United States Supreme Court. This is the final recourse. Unless it is a very special situation the case cannot be reopened in a lower appellate court.

The litigant can petition the Supreme Court to review any case. However, the Supreme Court is not required to consider all cases. In fact, it hears only a small percentage of the petitioned cases. The court's decision to review a case is purely discretionary, and its action is final. Because of the finality attached to its decisions, the Supreme Court is often termed the "Court of Last Resort."

We have described the basic framework within which the law operates. Remaining chapters examine specific areas of the law and practical legal problems that may arise in the course of an individual's daily activities.

Chapter Two

The Layman and the Courts

Most people think of the law solely in terms of professional lawyers, august judges, and complex statutes. Many forget that the individual citizen plays an important role in every legal action. As a party to a civil suit or as a defendant in a criminal prosecution, the individual is directly affected by the legal process. Trials could not take place if laymen did not serve as jurors and as witnesses. Furthermore, in most states, the individual can present a case in small claims court without the aid of an attorney. Although anyone can be involved in one of these situations, it is the legally informed individual who will know what to expect and how to proceed.

A layman as his own "lawyer"

At some time in his life, almost every individual is a victim of circumstances which would justify his taking another person to court. In most cases, litigation is impractical because the cost of going to court will be more than the sum involved. For example, suppose Jones hires Smith to repair an engine. Jones receives a bill for seventy-five dollars which he refuses to pay. Court costs and legal fees make it impractical for Smith to institute a legal action against Jones. Most likely he will bear the loss.

Most states recognize the frustrating problem presented by these situations. For many years they attempted to alleviate the problem through the Justice-of-the-Peace system. In general, this system proved to be a failure because it was disorganized, and because untrained individuals often presided over the proceedings.

The small claims court provided an answer. As former member of the Supreme Court Mr. Justice Roberts stated, the small claims court system is "an amazing story of progress toward the goal of equal justice for rich and poor." The purpose of the system is to provide a friendly forum for the litigation of cases that have high personal importance but involve little money.

A qualified judge presides over most small claims court proceedings. All such courts have jurisdictional limits. For example, the limit in the District of Columbia is $750. Thus, a person can file any case that involves an amount of $750 or less. Instead of the usual court costs, there is only a nominal filing fee of one or two dollars. Furthermore this can be waived under appropriate circumstances.

Perhaps the most appealing aspect of the system is that a party does not need to consult a lawyer. The form used to file a claim is simple. A knowledge of legal terms is unnecessary. The plaintiff—the person who starts the legal action—merely describes in his own words the basis of his claim against the defendant. If the individual requires assistance, the clerk of the court can provide it.

Frequent delays in bringing cases to trial have given rise to criticism of the American court system. The small claims court successfully avoids this problem. Hearings are usually scheduled two to three weeks after the claim is filed. This speed helps avoid the oft-quoted statement that "justice delayed is justice denied."

Unlike most legal actions, the small claims proceedings are conducted informally. In fact, the law distinctly requires the trial to be a simple procedure. For example, the rules for the District of Columbia small claims court are as follows:

> The parties and witnesses shall be sworn. The judge shall conduct the trial in such manner as to do substantial justice beween the parties according to the rules of substantive law, and shall not be bound by the provisions or rules of practice, procedure, pleading, or evidence, except such provisions relating to privileged communications.

In practice, the system operates as follows: At the start of the hearing, the person who filed the suit, or plaintiff, tells his story to the judge. The judge and the defendant then ask questions of the plaintiff. Next, witnesses relate their stories. If the defendant believes he is not responsible for the claim, he tells his side of the story. The judge does not proceed according to normal rules of evidence and procedure. Instead, his determination of the claim is based on substantial justice. Moreover, prompt and informal hearings insure that substantial justice is achieved.

Anyone interested in the particular rules applicable to his local small claims court can ask the local clerk of the court for information on the system as well as the proper forms to be used. This information will most likely provide the individual with enough legal knowledge to process his claim in this court.

Thus, the small claims court allows the individual to have his day in court without costs, without the need of a lawyer, and without becoming involved in the technical procedures that normally govern a legal proceeding.

The duties of a juror

The individual performs a vital function when he serves on a jury. In a sense, he insures the continuing operation of our court system. In a civil action tried by a jury, the jury determines whether the plaintiff or the defendant wins the law suit. If damages are to be awarded, the jury decides how much money the successful party receives. In criminal law, the jury must be persuaded beyond a reasonable doubt that the defendant is guilty before he can be convicted of the crime. The jury is therefore an independent fact-finder and an indispensable aid in maintaining the legal system as provided for by the United States Constitution.

In our legal system there are two kinds of juries: the petit or "petty" jury and the grand jury. The petit jury is a fact-finding body that decides civil cases and determines the guilt of an accused in a criminal trial. The grand jury is an accusatory body. It functions solely in criminal law. The grand jury hears preliminary prosecution evidence and determines whether that evidence is sufficient to indict or legally charge the person with a crime. When a grand jury indicts an individual, it charges him with a specific offense. The accused is then tried by a petit jury which determines his guilt or innocence of that charge. Thus, the two juries each have important functions to perform. This citizen-participation is the chief safeguard of the rights of the individual in relation to the state.

In general, a prospective juror must meet the following requirements: He must be a citizen of the United States between twenty-one and seventy years of age, in possession of his reasoning faculties, and in reasonably good health. However, the state laws governing jury qualifications vary.

In most states certain conditions automatically disqualify an individual from serving on a jury. For instance, a person convicted of a felony or of a misdemeanor involving moral turpitude (conduct contrary to honesty, justice, modesty, or good morals) cannot serve. The laws of many states specifically disqualify from jury duty members of a party or association which "advocates, advises, or teaches the duty, necessity or propriety of overthrowing or destroying the government by force or violence."

Some individuals are automatically exempted from jury duty because of their jobs. Thus, in many states, government officials are excluded from serving on a jury. Many others can claim exemption if they belong to professions that provide important public services. This list of people usually includes: surgeons, dentists, physicians, pharmacists, attorneys, priests, ministers, members of the military, policemen, firemen, and journalists. Individual states may have other classifications as to those who are not required to serve.

The method of compiling a list of prospective jurors differs among the various states. Some get the names of prospective jurors from voter registration lists. Other states draw from the tax assessment roles of the county. Some states also have a commissioner of jurors who determines which of the prospective jurors are competent and otherwise qualified to serve. These qualified jurors are sometimes called *veniremen*. When the petit jury is named at a trial, its members all come from the group of veniremen.

To choose the actual trial jurors from among the veniremen, lawyers conduct what is known as a *voir dire*. In other words, they question each venireman individually to determine whether he is qualified. For example, if the juror has prior knowledge of the case, personal prejudice, or is a blood relation of a party, he is disqualified from serving on that particular jury. When the lawyers for both sides are satisfied, the jury can be seated and the trial can begin.

The juror performs his all-important function during the trial. He must listen to all the evidence and determine which witnesses are telling the truth. At the end of the trial, the jury returns to its private room where it deliberates on the case and seeks to agree on a verdict. In his determination of the facts, the individual juror must make his decision in accordance with the instructions on the law given by the judge. Because compromises and other improper means of arriving at a verdict are occasionally employed the use of a jury has been criticized. However, no one can deny that the jury has proven an effective means to determine litigated questions among the nation's citizens.

Consequently, the individual should realize his duty to serve when he is called for jury duty. In criminal law, a trial by one's peers is a right in all but minor cases. In civil law, determination of the facts by a jury is a method with a long common law and constitutional heritage. The continuation of this form of justice will depend upon the performance of the individual.

The duties of a witness

Lawyers handle only the legal procedures of a trial and the substantive law involved. The individual witnesses provide the facts. This is an extremely important function, especially when one considers that a trial is nothing more than a forum in which each party, through its witnesses, is given a chance to tell his side of the story. After hearing all the testimony, the jury then decides which are the true facts.

It is clear that the individual witness has a significant bearing on the outcome of a trial. It is important, therefore, to know what is expected of a witness when he appears at a trial.

How does one become a witness? Simply put: Be in the right place at the right time. For example, two drivers, Sam Smith and Tom Jones, collided in the middle of an intersection. Besides the drivers, only one other person was present. John Donaldson was bicycling and happened to see the entire incident. Assuming that the question of liability for the accident comes to court, the testimony of Donaldson may prove conclusive.

Because of the common delay in bringing a case of this type to trial, often two or three years, Donaldson may have some difficulty in remembering his original impressions as to what, in his own view, actually took place. He will have to reject the tendency to supplement his memory with new and minute details so that his story is "complete." After going over his story several times, he may actually convince himself that these new particulars are true. However, the best witness is an honest witness. He is not afraid to say "I don't know" when cross-examined about additional possibilities and minutiae.

If a person witnesses an event which may become the subject of a lawsuit, he will soon find himself interviewed by attorneys or investigators from both sides. In some instances, one interview will take place with attorneys from both sides and will be recorded word for word. This is called a "deposition" and affords a fair method for the lawyers to discover the relevant facts. At the initial interview, the attorney representing the party for whom the individual is testifying will go over the facts with the witness. They will also discuss the format of the questions that will be asked on direct examination, sometimes question by question. The lawyer will attempt to prepare the witness for the type of questions he can expect during the cross-examination.

Juries determine facts both by what is said and by the manner in which it is said. As soon as a person takes the witness stand, the jurors, consciously or subconsciously, begin to formulate impressions on his credibility. There are many factors underlying these impressions:

- Whether the witness answers promptly or hesitates
- Whether he exaggerates
- Whether he is overbearing
- Whether he appears insincere
- Whether he is crude
- Whether he is obviously prejudiced toward one side

In addition, juries judge a witness by his physical appearance. Most juries composed of middle-Americans would not be fully objective toward a witness with long hair and exotic clothes. Also, a lawyer representing a woman in an alienation of affection lawsuit would be taking a risk if he permitted her to testify in a provocative dress. In spite of honest assertions to the contrary, such factors subconsciously affect the jury's impression of a witness. Commonly approved ideas for witnesses include good grooming; good posture; simple, clear explanations; sincerity; and honesty.

There is one question every witness should expect during cross-examination. Too often, the unprepared testimony goes like this:

Opposing lawyer:	"Have you talked to the plaintiff's lawyer about the facts you were going to relate in court"?
Witness:	"Uh, uh, ... No."

In this situation, the witness often is afraid that if he says "yes," it will appear that he and the lawyer have conspired to fabricate the facts. With little skill the opposing lawyer can force the witness into admitting that he lied and that he talked to the lawyer about the case. In point of fact it would be unprofessional for a lawyer to place a person on the witness stand without knowing the substance of his testimony. Thus, the prepared witness can answer, "yes" to this question without fearing that the weight of his testimony has been adversely affected. In fact, his own lawyer can use this situation to advantage by drawing out the facts of the interview and by revealing that its purpose was to clarify the facts and to prepare honest yet coherent testimony.

In summary, the layman is the best witness when he presents a respectable physical appearance, honestly relates the facts as he remembers them, does not fabricate to put together the loose ends of his memory, and gives clear, forthright answers.

The individual as a party in a civil lawsuit

At least two individuals are involved in every civil suit: a plaintiff and a defendant. These individuals are called "parties." The *plaintiff* is the person who files the complaint. This statement claims that the defendant is responsible for the plaintiff's damages. At trial, although the burden of proof is usually on the plaintiff, the defendant may have to defend himself against this claim. In some cases, he must show that he is not responsible for the injuries, either factually or legally. In other civil suits, the defendant must prove that it was the plaintiff's negligence that caused the injuries.

The parties in most civil trials are laymen. Many are unfamiliar with the legal technicalities of courtroom procedure. If the parties personally testify at the trial, the ideas expressed earlier about the responsibilities of witnesses are applicable.

The plaintiff and the defendant are directly affected by the outcome of a trial. One wins; the other loses, sometimes, substantial amounts of money. It is paramount, therefore, that each does everything within legal limits to help his cause.

Initially, a concerned party can best help himself by telling his lawyer everything remotely connected with his legal claim. Let the lawyer determine whether it is "legally relevant." Many individuals unwittingly damage their cases by leaving out "unimportant" details, only to discover later that those facts could have changed the verdict.

The initial interview should disclose the facts of the incident, including the names of witnesses, any documentary evidence, the weather if relevant, the sequence of events, and other details. The lawyer can investigate these facts and seek corroboration by other witnesses. This process slowly solidifies the case. If, after the initial interview, the individual recalls additional facts, he should inform his lawyer. However, the party should not talk to the opposing party, his attorney, or any investigator employed by the other person *unless his own lawyer is present.* The lawyer's presence can insure that the questioning is fair and relevant. If his lawyer is not there, an individual may be drawn into making misleading statements that could adversely affect his case.

At the trial itself, the party should present a neat appearance. Unconventional clothing can adversely affect a party just as it can a witness. In fact, he may lose his own case. Another important rule is to be concerned, but not insincere or overly emotional. Honesty and restraint are the party's best assets. Apart from giving any direct testimony, the plaintiff or defendant stays with his lawyer at the counsel's table and observes the trial. During the course of the proceedings, the lawyer may consult with him frequently to verify facts or to seek additional information. Apart from this information the job of the layman as a party is completed.

The individual as a criminal defendant

A defendant in a criminal proceeding is in an extremely hazardous position. An unfavorable verdict can put him in prison for months, years, or even life. Ignorance of the law is no defense in a criminal prosecution. The individual is *presumed* to have knowledge of the law. Therefore, individuals must become as knowledgeable of the law as possible. Consequently, a person will know what to expect if criminal charges are preferred against him.

The Bill of Rights in the United States Constitution expressly protects individuals from police-state tactics. Recent Supreme Court decisions have attempted to delineate the individual's rights. As a result, before the police can interrogate an individual, they must orally advise him of the following rights:

- He has a right to remain silent.
- Anything he says may be used against him in a court of law.
- He has a right to an attorney. If he cannot afford one, the state will appoint one, free of charge, to represent him before any questions are asked.

The individual, however, can *waive* or relinquish these rights. If he understands his rights yet decides to answer questions anyway, the individual's statements can be held against him in court.

Another constitutional provision often involved in criminal cases is the Fourth Amendment right against "unreasonable searches and seizures." Except when they make a search as a part of an arrest, the authorities generally need a search warrant before they can search an individual's premises. However, there are certain exceptional circumstances which preclude the need for a search warrant. One is the consent search.

An individual can consent to a search and thereby waive his Fourth Amendment rights. It must be remembered that evidence obtained in a search may be used against the individual if the case comes to trial. For example, many individuals attempt to bluff their way in hopes that the authorities will not find what they are looking for. If the article is found, there is little the individual can do since he consented to the search. In situations of this sort, the individual would be wise to withhold his consent and consult an attorney.

Assuming that the individual is brought to trial, what happens next?

One course would be to plead guilty to the charges. In general, an individual may wish to plead guilty if there is a solid case against him, if he has little or no defense, and if he hopes that a guilty plea will bring a lenient sentence.

It is imperative that the defendant understand the meaning and the effect of a guilty plea. By pleading guilty, the defendant judicially admits the crime and authorizes the judge to enter a conviction against him. In addition, the defendant waives, or gives up, three important rights:

- His Sixth Amendment right to be tried by a jury
- His Sixth Amendment right to confront the witnesses who would testify against him
- His Fifth Amendment right against self-incrimination

These are important rights, and only the defendant, in consultation with his attorney, can decide if he wishes to waive these rights by entering a guilty plea.

The defendant's other course of action is to plead not guilty. By pleading not guilty, the defendant requires the prosecution to convince the jury *beyond a reasonable doubt* that he is guilty of the offense. After the defendant has entered a plea of not guilty, the prosecution presents its case. The defense lawyer can present witnesses who support the defendant's claim of innocence. In addition the defendant may take the stand and give his own account. Whether or not the defendant testifies depends on the facts in that particular case.

However, it is important to remember that the Fifth Amendment guarantees the individual the right to remain silent. He cannot be made to incriminate himself. Thus, the defendant can refuse to take the stand. In fact, he can refuse to offer any evidence at all. Instead he may argue that the prosecution has failed to produce any conclusive evidence of his guilt. This may be a successful tactic. The law presumes the defendant to be innocent. Thus, if the state fails to prove its case, the defendant is acquitted.

In conclusion, the individual participates in court proceedings in a number of important ways. His relative success will depend on how he reacts to a specific situation. However, knowledge of the law and legal procedures coupled with adequate preparation are the best aids to a successful handling of court cases and duties.

Chapter Three

Lawsuits for Personal Injury

During the early development of the law, it was recognized that whenever possible the court should award compensation to those persons harmed by the actions of another. As a result of this determination, the theory of tort liability was conceived. Tort law is based on the idea that he who causes injury to another person or his property should be held responsible for that harm. It differs from criminal law, in which the state imposes punishment upon the guilty party and thereafter seeks to rehabilitate him. Tort theory is also different from contract law which the court uses to give legal effect to the promises of individuals.

Essentially a tort or civil wrong is the violation of a personal right guaranteed to the individual by law. A person has committed a tort if he has interfered with another person's safety, liberty, reputation, or private property. If the injured party can prove that the defendant proximately caused him harm, the court will hold the defendant responsible for the plaintiff's injury. If he does not have a valid defense, the defendant will be forced to pay for the damage he caused.

Tort liability can be divided into three broad areas:

- liability as a result of intentional conduct

- liability as a result of negligent conduct
- liability as a result of no fault conduct

Individual torts include such offenses as assault, battery, trespass, conversion, defamation, and deceit. In addition, accidental injuries caused by defective machinery or dangerous activities can render the owner or person in charge liable for the damage.

Since the individual can easily become involved in a tortious situation, often through little or no fault of his own, it is useful to know what actions are considered torts and what defenses exist to eliminate or reduce liability.

Liability resulting from intentional conduct

An individual has committed an intentional tort if he has knowingly violated the rights of another. He may have considered his action a practical joke, or he may have believed that no harm would result. Neither excuse constitutes a valid defense. He will be held liable for an intentional tort because he desired to wrongfully interfere with another's interests and because he acted upon this desire. If the guilty party is a legally responsible person and if he has injured his victim, he will be forced to compensate that individual for his injuries.

Since many seemingly harmless pranks or thoughtless actions can lead to liability for a civil wrong, it is useful to know what acts constitute intentional torts.

Assault. Most lawyers define assault as an intentional act which provokes in the victim a reasonable apprehension that the aggressor intends and is able to harm him. No contact is necessary. The harm is the mental fear of injury. To illustrate, suppose two neighbors, Jones and Smith, are always quarreling. Jones starts to build a garage which Smith believes will infringe on his property. In his anger, Smith grabs a hatchet. Running toward Jones, he begins yelling and waving the hatchet wildly. Although Smith does not actually hit Jones, he may be liable for assault because his acts placed Jones under a reasonable fear that he would be injured. Even if Smith meant no harm and was only carrying a practical joke to an extreme, the liability still exists.

An assault action, however, presupposes that the victim is *aware* of the impending harm. Suppose that Smith was behind Jones when he raised the hatchet. At this point, there is no assault because Jones is unaware of the raised hatchet. He has no apprehension of impending harm. Or, if Smith points a gun at Jones, but Jones does not see it, the result is the same. No liability exists because the victim is unaware of the act and therefore cannot be frightened or intimidated.

Normally, words alone are insufficient to constitute an assault. The aggressor must have some ability to carry out the impending harm. Thus, *words coupled with an overt act* are sufficient. For example, if Allen approaches Baker, waves a pistol at him, and says "stick'em up," he has committed an assault. The words alone are no cause for fear, but the words, coupled with the pistol, constitute a distinct threat. In this situation, Baker's fear that he will be harmed is entirely reasonable.

Battery. In simple terms a battery is a completed assault. It can be defined as the unjustified use of force against the body of another person, resulting in unconsented contact with that person. Fear or apprehension of injury is not part of this tort. All that is necessary is that the force be inten-

tional and that it be applied without the victim's consent. In our example, if Smith had actually struck Jones with the hatchet, he would have committed a battery upon him and would be liable for any resulting injuries.

Battery sometimes occurs as the result of unauthorized surgical operations. Suppose Dr. Casey is to perform an operation on Mrs. Olson's right leg. Permission is granted for that operation, but while in the operating room, Dr. Casey discovers an ugly tumor on his patient's left leg and removes it. Courts have held that since he did not have permission to operate on the left leg, the doctor is liable for battery. In view of these court results, hospitals often insert a protective clause in their consent forms. This clause gives them permission to perform any additional surgery that is both beneficial and minor. Therefore, it is important to read a consent form for an operation carefully in order to see what clauses it contains. If a question arises about the meaning of a particular statement, the doctor can usually answer it. The safer course of action, however, might be to ask a lawyer to explain the meaning and effect of the clause.

False imprisonment. False imprisonment is a violation of the individual's right of personal liberty. This tort is described as the unlawful and unjustified detention of a person against his will. The law considers a person falsely imprisoned only if he is completely prevented from going about his business. A victim of this tort can bring an action against the person responsible and recover money compensation for his loss of time, any physical injury, illness, or any mental anguish he may have suffered.

A common situation which may result in a legal action for false imprisonment is the following:

> Mr. Jones, a private citizen, rents a policeman's uniform and confronts Adams whom he does not like. Upon hearing that he is "under arrest," Adams submits to Jones's purported authority. Jones is liable to Adams for false imprisonment.

In their attempts to curb shoplifting, store merchants occasionally violate the personal liberty of suspects by detaining them without a reasonable cause, as in the following example:

> Mr. Davis, the store detective, stops Jimmy and Johnny as they try to leave the store. Davis did not see the boys take anything nor did anyone report to him that they did. He just does not trust their looks or their mannerisms as they wander through the store. His examination of their shopping bags shows that they have paid for everything. Johnny and Jimmy could file a lawsuit against Davis for false arrest and illegal confinement.

Shoplifting is such a major problem that many states have modified their laws governing false imprisonment. These new provisions allow authorized store personnel to detain a person whom they reasonably believe has stolen some merchandise. For example, if a clerk informed Davis that Jimmy and Johnny had slipped some articles under their coats, Davis could detain them for a reasonable length of time to conduct an investigation. Under the modified law, Davis would not be liable for false imprisonment if the subsequent search failed to reveal stolen merchandise.

Trespass. Strictly speaking, a trespass is the unlawful invasion of another person's real property. This tort has its roots in early English and American common law. Traditionally, the individual has enjoyed the right to own and use land without interference. Thus, a person who intentionally enters private property without the owner's consent technically commits trespass, regardless of whether he harms the property. Common examples of technical trespass include animals intruding on one's property, people using private property as a short cut, or children throwing rocks on someone's land. Since the harm to the land is minimal in these cases, a court would probably award nominal damages, such as one dollar.

Minor trespasses are relatively unimportant when compared to situations resulting in serious damage to the land or its owner. For example, the driver of a moving van, while attempting to turn around in the street, drives the truck over the curb onto a private lawn and crushes the owner's new sidewalk. The company is liable to the property owner for the damage. To illustrate another serious trespass, suppose some neighborhood children camp on the far end of a man's acreage without his consent. Thinking that they have put out their camp fire, the children bed down for the night. However, the wind comes up and fans the coals to life. The subsequent fire spreads and eventually burns down the owner's home. He can recover damages from the children and possibly from their parents for the loss of his home.

Error is no excuse in the eyes of the law. A trespass committed by mistake is still a trespass, and the transgressor is liable to the property owner for any damage he has caused. For example, John and George have the mineral rights to a parcel of land on which they discover natural gas. After capping their find, they seek a method of economically producing it. Meanwhile, ABC Gas Company, under the apprehension that it is drilling on its own land, "discovers" and attempts to recoup the same natural gas deposit. Since John and George have the legal rights to the minerals, they can recover for damages although ABC Gas Company believed that it was drilling on its own land.

Conversion. Trespass applies to the intentional invasion of real property. In a similar manner, conversion refers to the exercise of dominion over someone else's personal property. Personal property includes tangible possessions such as cars, appliances, clothing, and jewelry, and intangible property such as stocks and bonds.

The term conversion encompasses several different acts. One is the unauthorized appropriation, either openly or fraudulently, of another's property.

> John, a college student, goes into Joe's room and takes his typewriter. Joe has not given his permis-

sion for this act. Since he had no right to take the machine, John is liable to Joe for conversion.

> Mr. Slick, a con-artist, convinces Mrs. Simpson to give him $2,000 worth of stock certificates as an investment in his uranium venture. There is no such venture. Mr. Slick is liable to Mrs. Simpson for conversion.

Another form of conversion is the unauthorized use of property. Under this principle a person legally acquires possession of the property but subsequently converts it to his own personal use without the owner's permission.

> Mr. Porter drives into Acme Parking Company for off-street parking during business hours. Instead of parking the car, the parking attendant drives it around all day. Since Mr. Porter gave no consent for this use, the parking attendant is liable to Mr. Porter for conversion.

Another illustration of this tort is the unlawful destruction or alteration of property owned by another. When a person destroys another's property, the damage is obvious. It is a more difficult problem when the property is altered or changed.

> Mr. Stone takes his light tan suit to Ace Cleaners for dry-cleaning. Instead of cleaning it, Ace Cleaners dyes the suit a dull black color. Ace Cleaners is liable to Mr. Stone for conversion.

> Mr. Pane has a cord of large logs in the backyard. He plans to construct a fence with these logs. While Mr. Pane is away, Sam enters the yard and cuts the logs into small pieces, suitable only for firewood. This alteration of the identity of Pane's property renders Sam liable to Mr. Pane for the wrongful conversion of the logs.

Conversion also occurs when an individual disposes of property without the owner's consent. Mr. Dix lends Mr. Dent his diamond stick pin. Without Mr. Dix's permission, Mr. Dent gives it to a third party. Mr. Dent is liable for converting the pin to his own use.

A refusal to surrender property upon demand of the owner is also a form of conversion.

> Mr. Lewis hires Acme Moving & Storage to transport his furniture across the country and then keep it in storage for a month. Upon finding a new house, Mr. Lewis demands his furniture. Acme, for no reason, refuses to surrender the goods. Acme is liable for conversion.

However, if the demand is unreasonable, there is no liability. Suppose Mr. Lewis demanded immediate delivery at 2:30 a.m. In this case, there is no liability. Also, when there is a legitimate question as to the identity of the man who demands delivery, there may be no liability on the part of Acme.

The act of conversion is complete when the actor takes, detains, or disposes of the item of property. At this point, the victim has the right to bring an action for conversion in court. If the owner subsequently recovers possession of the item, he can bring an action, but the amount of recovery will be decreased because he has recovered the object of the suit.

Defenses. If an individual has a defense to an intentional tort, he will not have to pay damages. The law will leave the victim as it found him. The more common defenses to intentional torts are privilege, consent, self-defense, defense of property, and legal justification.

The law applies the term "privilege" to those situations in which the defendant, although otherwise liable, has acted in the public interest. He is therefore entitled to freedom from any liability, even at the expense of damage or injury to the victim. One example would be the store owner who is privileged to detain suspected shoplifters in order to curtail this crime.

Privilege sometimes serves as a defense to battery. An immigration doctor who injects preventive shots in every incoming passenger to safeguard the health of the country's inhabitants is acting under a privilege. Hence he is not liable for the unconsented contact with a passenger's body.

Another defense is "consent," meaning that the victim "consented" to the act. For example, participants in sports consent to playing. If their bodies are touched, there is no tort. If two belligerents start to fight, most courts say that each consented to fight. Therefore, neither can recover from the other for any injuries he may have incurred in the *mêlée*. Under the same theory, a surgical operation usually requires consent in order to protect the doctor from liability for battery.

The privilege of "self-defense" is based on the necessity of giving a man the right to take reasonable steps to defend himself. The right to act in self-defense exists not only when the danger is real, but also when it is reasonably apparent that danger exists. A common situation allowing this defense occurs when an individual accosts another in an alley and tries to take that person's wallet. If the victim reasonably believes that his safety is threatened, he may use reasonable force to fend off his attacker. When he no longer faces any danger the individual cannot inflict further harm upon his attacker. Instead, he must seek the law's help.

The defense of private property is subject to the same rules that govern self-defense of one's person. An individual may use a reasonable amount of force to safeguard the peaceful possession and enjoyment of his property. A person cannot use excessive force. For example, a rifle should not be used to ward off intruders when it is apparent that an oral command to leave would be sufficient.

"Legal justification" is the defense that protects all law enforcement officers who are acting in the line of duty. Their acts in apprehending suspects cannot be the basis for an intentional tort. Thus, a search of an individual's premises conducted with a valid search warrant would not support a claim of trespass. The officer was legally justified in entering the property.

Liability resulting from negligent conduct

Court cases arising from negligence are by far the most common form of tort suit today. This is perhaps because most automobile suits involve questions of negligence.

The essential prerequisites to a successful negligence suit are these:

- An existing duty to use proper care and attention in a certain situation
- Conduct which lacks the proper care and diligence that can reasonably be expected under the circumstances
- A reasonably close relationship between the cause and the effect
- No defense to the action
- Damage resulting from the action

In order to sustain an action, a person's conduct must be negligent. This can be defined as conduct which falls below a reasonable standard.

It is important to remember that not every negligent act results in liability. The act must proximately cause the injury. For example, "A" signals to make a left turn. The driver behind "A" suddenly swerves and runs into a third car. "A" may not be liable for that accident. Although the accident might not have occurred if "A" had not signaled to turn, most courts would say that "A's" act was too tangential and remote from the injury. Therefore, "A" would not be liable for any damage. (Defenses available in a negligence lawsuit will be discussed later in the chapter.)

Most of the litigation surrounding negligence suits concerns whether the conduct is negligent. For purposes of discussion, negligent conduct will be separated into three general areas:

- Harm directly caused by a negligent act
- Harm caused by a failure to act

• Harm caused by an instrumentality, controlled by another

Harm directly caused by a negligent act. In this area, harm is caused by an affirmative but negligent act. In other words, the individual fails to exercise reasonable care and caution while performing a certain act. For example, a department store delivery man comes to your home to deliver a large package. While carrying it through the front door, he misjudges the distance and breaks the glass in the door. His act lacks the reasonable care that can be expected under the circumstances. Accordingly, he is liable

for the broken pane.

Another circumstance which can result in liability for negligence is the "misplaced sponge" situation.

> Mrs. Jones is to have an operation for an appendectomy. After the operation is completed, the hospital staff discovers that one of the surgical sponges is missing. Subsequent investigation establishes that the sponge was left in Mrs. Jones's body during the operation. This conduct is negligent. Mrs. Jones may be able to recover from the hospital and possibly from the doctor.

The grounds for recovery in this case stem from society's belief that it is negligent conduct to surgically operate and leave a sponge in the patient. An interesting sidelight to this tort action is the question of proof. Because she was unconscious, it would be impossible for the patient to testify positively that a negligent act occurred during the operation. Thus, to allow the patient to recover damages, the law utilizes the principle of *res ipsa loquitur*. This Latin phrase, literally meaning "the thing speaks for itself," permits a jury to infer negligence by the circumstances of the situation. Applied to the example it means that sponges are not, in the absence of negligence, left inside patients. Moreover, since no one else had access to the patient's stomach, it can be inferred that the doctor, the hospital, or both acted negligently in the conduct of the operation. This theory permits the patient to recover for the damages she sustained.

The majority of Americans drive or ride in automobiles. As a result, automobile suits are among the most frequently heard cases in court. Moreover, almost all suits arising from automobile accidents involve questions of negligence. Since paying for property damage and personal injuries can reach astronomical proportions, the question of who is liable for the damages is crucial.

The law imposes a duty on the automobile operator to drive with a reasonable amount of care and in a manner

which does not interfere with the rights of others. If the driver's conduct does not measure up to this reasonable standard, it will be labeled as negligent. The driver will be liable for any injuries resulting from his conduct. For example, while driving along the highway, "A" falls asleep at the wheel. His car crosses the median and collides with "B" who was driving in a reasonable manner. Based on these facts, "A" is liable to "B" for any personal injuries and any property damage to "B's" car.

That is the simple situation. In an actual case, the individual laws of a particular state may prescribe additional rules. The laws in some states, such as New York, Iowa, Michigan, and California, hold the owner of the car responsible for any damages when the car is being operated with his consent. In states that have the "family-car doctrine," the head of the household is liable for the negligent driving of any member of his home. Nearly half the states have "guest statutes" which prevent a passenger from recovering for injuries caused by his host unless he can prove that his host's conduct was reckless as opposed to negligent. Because of the difficulty of proving reckless conduct, or gross negligence as it is sometimes called, many passengers are barred from recovering any damages. In addition, there are several theories, to be discussed later, that provide a defense to a negligence suit. These numerous twists in the law make it imperative that a person involved in an accident be fully aware of its legal implications.

Harm caused by a failure to act. A person may be liable for injuries due to negligence when he has a duty to act and fails to do so.

In the early development of law, the courts distinguished between nonfeasance and misfeasance. Individuals had no duty to protect or aid others, but if they so attempted and failed, they were liable for misfeasance. More recently courts have imposed upon individuals the duty to act when they are in a special relation to the victim. For example, an individual is not required by law to save a person who is drowning in a public waterhole. However, if the pool is located on his property, the landowner is obliged to make a reasonable attempt to save a person who appears to be drowning.

The law also specifies that common carriers, such as railroad and airline personnel, innkeepers and hotel managers, have a duty to act in situations involving members of the public. For example, a railroad has a duty to aid any passengers who become ill. If the railroad does not offer its help, it will be held liable for damages by aggravation of the illness. Under the same principle, innkeepers have a duty to respond to the emergencies of their guests.

The law does not always require individuals to help one another. However, if a person tries to help someone in a perilous situation and, in the process, commits a negligent act, he is liable for the resulting aggravation of the injury. Suppose John Smith sees that Jimmy Jones is stuck in an escalator. Mr. Smith frees Jimmy, takes him to an isolated room and leaves him there without seeking further help. Mr. Smith might be liable to Jimmy for any resulting harm. Although Mr. Smith was under no obligation to free Jimmy from the escalator, he assumed that duty. Consequently, he incurred a further duty to properly and reasonably care for him. He had no right to prevent further help by leaving Jimmy in a deserted room.

Harm caused by an instrumentality controlled by another. Under this broad rule an individual in control of a machine or instrumentality is liable for damages to any person injured by that instrumentality. One clear example is the store owning the escalator that injured Jimmy. A similar situation would occur if an elevator cable broke because of negligent inspection and caused injuries to the passengers. The owner of the store and/or the elevator inspection company would be liable for the resulting injuries.

Under this same principle, managers are responsible for negligent acts committed by their employes or agents. Suppose Acme Gravel Company delivers a load of crushed stone to Mr. Olson's driveway. While completing the delivery the truck driver negligently backs into Mr. Olson's boat. Acme, which has control and is responsible for its driver, would be liable to Mr. Olson for the damage to the boat. In another example, a bottling company would be liable to the individual consumer if its bottling machine processed a full bottle which contained some harmful foreign matter. Since the company is in control of the machine, and since it is impossible for the foreign matter to come from another source, the company is liable for damages incurred by the consumer.

Defenses. There are several defenses which are applicable to all three areas of negligent conduct. Each of these either erases or lessens the amount of liability. Essentially, there are four doctrines which constitute a complete or partial defense to liability for damages caused by negligent conduct:

- Contributory negligence
- Assumption of the risk
- Last clear chance
- Comparative negligence

Under the theory of *contributory negligence,* if the person bringing suit for negligence damages has acted negligently himself, he is precluded from any recovery. This rule applies in almost all states. It is best illustrated by an example below.

Assume the following facts in this situation: Although it is a rainy night, Mr. Jones is not watching the road carefully. As a result he crosses the median strip of the highway and crashes head-on into Mr. Smith's car. However, Mr. Smith did not have his headlights or windshield wipers on, nor was he paying attention to the traffic. Thereafter, Mr. Smith sues Mr. Jones on the theory that Jones acted negligently when he crossed the median. According to Smith, this act resulted in his personal injury and harm to his property.

At the trial, Mr. Jones defends himself on the theory that Mr. Smith was contributorily negligent. In other words, Smith's failure to pay attention and to turn on his wipers and headlights was unreasonable under the circumstances and therefore contributed to the accident. Under this set of facts, the theory of contributory negligence could be applied successfully.

Under the laws of most states, the existence of contributory negligence bars any recovery. This rule is based on the theory that a person should not be permitted to recover in a lawsuit when his own conduct partially contributed to the injury.

The defense of contributory negligence cannot be applied to an intentional tort. For example, if "A" commits a battery upon "B," "A" cannot defend by alleging that "B's" conduct negligently helped to bring about the act.

On the other hand, if the plaintiff is suing under the theory that the other person was acting recklessly, a more serious offense, then a defense of contributory negligence would not preclude his recovery. Suppose in our earlier example that Mr. Jones was drunk while driving. This is a strong indication of reckless conduct. The fact that Mr. Smith was contributorily negligent would not prevent him from recovering for the reckless conduct or gross negligence of Mr. Jones.

Assumption of the risk means that a person, with full knowledge of the risk of possible harm, voluntarily undertakes a course of action that might cause him injury. If he is later injured by that action, he cannot recover because he knew the risks of injury, yet agreed to take his own chances. One of the most common applications of this defense occurs in connection with sports events. Courts consistently have held that spectators assume the risk of being hit by a foul ball, a flying puck, or errant golf balls. As Judge Cardozo once said: "The timorous may stay at home."

In another case, suppose Baker offers Dan a ride in his hot rod but tells him that one tire is extremely weak and may blow out very soon. If knowing this risk, Dan accepts the ride, he will have assumed any risk of injury. The tire does in fact blow, the car rolls over, and both persons are injured. Dan will be unable to recover from Baker because, knowing the danger of a blowout, he fully consented to the ride.

An important fact to remember about assumption of the risk is that it can be a defense in situations where contributory negligence does not apply. For example, a person injures another through gross negligence or reckless conduct. If the victim assumed the risk of injury, he cannot recover damages. Simple contributory negligence on the victim's part would not bar recovery. To illustrate, suppose Harry is driving while extremely drunk. Mike is fully aware of Harry's condition yet he voluntarily accepts a ride. If Mike is subsequently injured by Harry's conduct, he will be unable to recover. Although Harry's conduct was reckless, Mike assumed the risk. Assumption of the risk is also a valid defense against a suit involving an intentional tort, such as assault or battery.

Many people tend to confuse contributory negligence with assumption of the risk. It is an understandable error since both defenses prevent the plaintiff from recovering damages.

As can be seen, there is usually a distinct difference between conduct constituting assumption of the risk and that known as contributory negligence. Contributory negligence usually involves no knowledge of any risk. It is merely negligent conduct. Assumption of the risk is reasonable conduct insofar as it is probable that no harm will result. Attending a sports event is one example. However, there is an area of conduct in which the two overlap. This is commonly called an unreasonable assumption of the risk. A person who voluntarily consents to ride with a drunken driver is guilty of both contributory negligence and assumption of the risk.

Because many people were dissatisfied with the harsh rulings that often resulted in cases involving contributory negligence, the rule has been modified to include the doctrine of *last clear chance.* Under this theory, the last person who could avoid the injury or damage is liable. This doctrine covers essentially two situations. In the first, the plaintiff, because of some negligent conduct on his part, places himself in a helpless condition. The defendant notices this situation in time to avoid it, fails to avoid it, and causes injury to the plaintiff. Despite the plaintiff's contributory negligence, courts permit him to recover under the theory that the defendant had the last clear chance to avoid the accident. Suppose Williams is riding his bicycle through a busy intersection. He falls, due to his own negligence, and the bike lands on him. Townsend, who is driving toward the intersection, sees Williams lying helpless in the street yet runs over him. Since Townsend could have avoided the accident, Williams is permitted to recover from Townsend under the theory of last clear chance.

The second situation involves an "inattentive plaintiff." In this case the victim is able to escape. The defendant, aware of the danger and able to avoid the plaintiff, still injures him. The defendant is liable to the plaintiff under the doctrine of last clear chance. To illustrate, Jones stops his car on a railroad trestle to observe the view. He does not see a train coming from the opposite direction. The railroad engineer, negligently thinking that Jones will move on, does not blow his whistle. Furthermore, instead of stopping the train, the engineer proceeds through the crossing and injures Jones. Although Jones was negligent in his failure to pay proper attention, he will be permitted to recover from the railroad because the engineer had the last opportunity to avoid the accident.

The doctrine of *comparative negligence* is similar in origin to the doctrine of last clear chance. It also was developed to alleviate court rulings against an injured party who negligently contributed to his own injury. Generally provided by statute, this doctrine seeks to apportion the recovery of money in accordance with the degree to which each party was negligent. For example, if "A's" negligence is found to be twice "B's" negligence, "B" would recover two-thirds of the damages he suffered. This doctrine exists in only a handful of states, including Nebraska, Wisconsin, South Dakota, Arkansas, and Illinois. The doctrine works as follows:

> "A" is injured in an accident with "B." "B" is sued by "A." The jury determines that "A's" damages total $100,000 and that "B's" negligence accounted for two-thirds of the damages. Accordingly, "A" would recover $67,000 from "B."

Liability resulting from no fault conduct

We have already examined intentional interferences and negligent conduct. In the area of no fault liability, neither party has intentionally interfered with another's person or property, nor was either party's conduct below the reasonable standard. Yet liability is imposed upon one of the parties. Why? The reason lies in a policy determination made by the court. In effect, the court asked: As between the two parties, who should bear the loss?

Common situations of no fault liability include injuries caused by abnormally dangerous instrumentalities or activities, and the application of the "Dram Shop" laws. The first situation involves injuries inflicted by animals. Liability is imposed on the owner of the animal because it is felt that he should be required to protect the community from any risks involved in keeping that animal. Most courts hold that damages to property caused by the trespass of animals such as horses, cattle, and wandering fowls impose strict liability on their owners. Some courts make an exception to this rule for cats and dogs since they cause minimal damage in their wanderings. On the other hand, statutes in many states expressly provide that owners are liable for damage done by all domestic animals.

Courts have consistently held that any injury inflicted by a "dangerous animal" subjects the owner of that animal to strict liability. Lions, tigers, bears, monkeys, and similar species are classed as "dangerous." When other animals inflict injury, the law imposes liability only if the owner of the animal knew, or had reason to know, that the animal might be dangerous. This class includes cattle, sheep, horses, dogs, and cats. It is from this rule that the old phrase "every dog is entitled to one bite" received its validity. Presumably after the first bite, the owner should know that his dog has a propensity to become violent and attack someone. If at some later date the dog injures a third party, its owner may be held responsible for the damages.

Strict liability for damages is imposed on the owners of abnormally dangerous instrumentalities or the directors of dangerous activities. Under this theory, the owner of a ten-ton tractor or steam roller is held liable for any injuries caused by these machines. Dynamite blasting is an example of an abnormally dangerous activity that can impose liability on the person in charge. Liability has been imposed in these situations, in part, because the owner of a potentially dangerous machine or the controller of a hazardous activity is seeking economic gain through its use. Therefore, he should pay for any injuries which occur as a consequence of his operations.

Strict liability is also imposed in those situations involving the "Dram Shop" laws. Many states have statutes holding sellers of intoxicants responsible for any injuries to a third person resulting from the intoxication of a customer. For example, suppose Roger buys a large amount of liquor from Rush's Tavern. As a consequence, Roger becomes extremely intoxicated and later incites a brawl in which he injures John. Under the "Dram Shop" laws, John could recover damages from Rush's Tavern for the injuries he suffered as a result of Roger's intoxication.

Deceit

Deceit is a misrepresentation that interferes with a person's interests. An individual is liable for deceit when he deliberately cheats another person of property or some other interest by misstating or omitting relevant facts. The following elements must be present in a law suit brought to recover damages for deceit:

- The defendant must make a false statement.
- The defendant must know that it is false.
- It must be made with the intention of inducing the victim to act or refrain from acting.
- The victim must justifiably rely on the defendant's misrepresentation in acting or in refraining from acting.
- The victim must suffer damages as a result of his reliance.

To illustrate this tort, suppose Jones, purporting to be an insurance salesman, calls on Smith and seeks to sell him fire insurance on his new home. Jones tells Smith that he can write a valid binder, insuring the home against loss by fire. Jones deliberately makes this statement in the hope of defrauding Smith of some "premium" payments. Not having any reason to be suspicious, Smith relies on Jones's statements and writes him a check for the first "premium." Thereafter, fire destroys Smith's home and he has no insurance. Smith could recover from Jones for damages he incurred due to Jones's misrepresentations.

Defamation

A person has been defamed when a communication is made to others which tends to expose him to public hatred, shame, ostracism, ridicule, or which causes him to be avoided or shunned. There are two forms of defamatory communication: libel or written communications, and slander which is an oral statement.

Any time a defamatory communication is printed, the victim can recover without proving any particular personal injury. The existence of damages is conclusively presumed from the publication of the libel. By the same reasoning, slander results any time a defamatory communication is made orally. Generally, however, in the case of slander, the victim must allege damages in order to have a case tried in court.

Truth is always a defense to a libel or slander suit. However, a mistaken belief that the printed matter is true does not constitute a defense. Consent is another defense. If the person who claims to have been defamed actually consented to the publication of the statement, he cannot recover damages.

Judges, legislators and executive officials are *privileged* to make defamatory statements during the exercise of their duties. However, this privilege is balanced by the rule allowing individuals to comment fairly on the actions of public officials. Liability for libel or slander will not be imposed upon the person making the comment unless the public official can prove it was made with "actual malice."

Personal involvement in a tortious situation

Many of the basic principles of tort law have been discussed in this chapter. Individual situations, however, may require additional principles or variations of the basic rules. Thus, the individual should consult a competent attorney before making any decision in these matters. In most situations involving tort liability, the incident happens very quickly and the parties act impulsively.

Since this type of action can be detrimental to a person's interests, the best rule is to be prepared. If he recognizes the possible consequences of the situation, the individual can minimize his injuries and maximize his chances of recovering from the responsible party. People involved in accidents often find that impulsive statements such as "it was all my fault" come back to haunt them if they are charged with negligent conduct. They may find out that, legally, it was their fault. In light of these many unfortunate incidents, remember to gather the following information if you are involved in a tortious situation:

1. The date and hour of the incident
2. The exact place of the incident
3. The names, addresses, and phone numbers of all witnesses
4. The weather conditions, if applicable
5. Pictures of relevant data, if possible
6. Any statements made by a witness or a participant
7. Name and address of any attending physician, if applicable
8. A brief, written, summary of exactly what occurred during the incident

In addition, it is best to make no statement whatsoever. The better course is to make a short reply to any question or to refuse to comment without first speaking to a lawyer. Using these recommendations can prove invaluable if the case goes to court over injuries resulting from the incident.

Chapter Four

When You Make a Contract

People enter into contracts every day. Most are simple affairs, prompt transactions that are soon forgotten. Ordering a newspaper or magazine creates a contract. Agreeing to buy a new or used automobile binds the purchaser to a contract. Credit accounts are premised on the existence of a contract. Even using the telephone or turning on a radio implies an acceptance of one's legal obligation to pay the telephone and electric utilities for the service they provide.

Generally defined, a contract is a promise which creates a legal obligation. A contract seldom presents legal difficulties and rarely does it require litigation in court. However, an occasional legal problem can arise. These difficult contracts create the legal cases comprising the law of contracts. The concerned individual is in a better position to avoid legal problems in his personal and business affairs if he is aware of these basic contract principles.

Essentially, a contract is a promise that can be enforced by a court of law. Most often, it is an agreement between two or more persons in which each promises to do or not to do a certain act. Once a contract is created, each person has a duty to perform that act which he promised to do. If one party fails to carry out his promise, the other has a legal right to go into court and seek one of two remedies. He can ask to be awarded damages, the monetary amount equal to the injury he has suffered because the other party broke his promise, or "specific performance," a direct command from the court ordering the other party to carry out his promise.

The principles and examples given in this chapter will explain each of the elements of an enforceable contract.

Essentials of a contract

To be valid and enforceable, a contract must be an agreement made by two or more persons who are legally capable of entering into a contract. It consists of an offer, an acceptance of that offer, and promises supported by "consideration." In addition, there must be no law declaring the agreement null and void.

Legal capacity to contract. In order for a contract to be legally binding, the persons making the contract must be capable of entering into such an agreement. In other words, they must have the "legal capacity to contract." If they are not legally capable, the contract is unenforceable, and sometimes null and void. However, there is an important distinction between the two results. If one or both of the parties is legally incapacitated, the contract may in some instances be void; in other instances it may be voidable. When a person has been declared legally insane, any contract he enters into is *void.* The agreement is not legally binding because his guardian has possession and control of all his property rights and business interests, including his right and ability to enter into a contract.

In most other instances, the contract is voidable. Thus, if one of the parties has a partial legal infirmity, he can avoid the legal effect of a previous agreement. Examples of limited legal incapacity include minors, drunks, and insane persons who have not yet been legally determined. The contracts of a minor, in most states a person under twenty-one, are voidable at his option. However, the minor retains his right to hold the adult to his contract.

> Jimmy, age 17, signs a contract with Dick's Used Car Lot to purchase a '51 jalopy. After signing the contract, he decides against the purchase. He can legally avoid the contract by telling the salesman that he is a minor. Suppose, however, that, after the contract is signed, the salesman determines that the car is worth twice the value of the amount in the contract. The salesman cannot avoid the performance of the contract because Jimmy is a minor. He is bound by the terms of the agreement which Jimmy can fully enforce against the used car lot.

There are some exceptions that alleviate the harshness of this one-sided rule. Thus, a minor will be held liable for the necessaries furnished him. To illustrate: Jimmy, in need of essential clothing, signs a contract for several outfits. If these items are necessary, he cannot later avoid liability by pleading that he is a minor. He will still be liable for the reasonable value of the clothing. In many states a minor is also held responsible for his contracts when he misrepresents to the other party that he is an adult, and his appearance supports the statement. Jimmy goes into Acme Jeweler's and states that he is twenty-two years old. The owner decides that he looks at least twenty-three. They then sign a contract for the purchase of a $200 ring. Since the owner reasonably relied on the minor's statements, Jimmy may not be permitted to avoid liability by pleading that he is a minor. Jimmy may be held to his contract although he is under the legal age to contract.

An insane person who enters into a contract can avoid its performance after he has regained his reasoning powers. He can also avoid liability while he is temporarily insane if his legal representative files a notice that the contract will not be performed.

A person who enters a contract while drunk also has a power of avoidance. This is based on the theory that his drunkenness rendered him incapable of understanding the nature and effect of a contract. Therefore, he is permitted, at his option, to avoid the terms of an otherwise legal and binding contract.

Offer. The person who makes the offer to contract is called the "offeror." The person to whom it is addressed is called the "offeree." An offer is a promise, but it is a promise conditioned by the acceptance of the offeree. An offer must promise the performance or nonperformance of a specific act. The essential terms of the offer must be stated, and the offeree must be aware of the offer.

> Jones says to Smith: "If you promise to write a book, I promise to give you $10,000." Smith makes that promise. Jones's statement is an offer. Smith's acceptance creates a legally enforceable contract.

It must be remembered that an offer is not the same as a "preliminary negotiation." If Sam's Sports Shop has a tennis racket with a ten dollar price tag in its window, this does not constitute an offer to sell. It is merely an "invitation" to come in and negotiate further. In this case, it would be the customer who actually makes the offer by saying, in effect, "If you give me that tennis racket, I will give you ten dollars."

Another requirement for a valid offer is that the terms of the offer be stated definitely. If the terms are too indefinite there can be no acceptance and therefore no contract. If Able says to Baker, "Work for me, and I will give you a share of the profits of the business," Able has not made a valid offer because the terms of employment are too vague. No objective standard can be used to determine a "share" of the profits. Therefore, any attempted acceptance of that statement would not create an enforceable contract.

An offer is not valid forever. If it is withdrawn before someone accepts, a later attempted "acceptance" will not create a contract. However, the notice of withdrawal must be made known to the same people as was the offer. Once they are aware of its withdrawal, they can no longer legally accept the offer.

The offer usually terminates upon the expiration of a reasonable time, normally three months, or upon the expiration of its express terms, "This offer is valid through June 30, 1971." The offer may be terminated before either of these times under the following conditions:

- Express withdrawal by the offeror
- Express rejection by the offeree
- The death of the offeror
- Passage of a law that makes the proposed contract illegal

Occasionally, the offeror will unearth new facts that increase the value of the property he has offered to sell. As a result he may withdraw his offer:

> Jones offers to sell his farm for $500 per acre to Murphy. Before Murphy has decided whether or not to accept the offer, Jones discovers oil on the property and decides that he does not want to sell the property at the earlier price. Once Murphy is aware of this fact, he can no longer legally accept Jones's previous offer. The offer has been withdrawn.

The offer would also be terminated if Jones died before Murphy was able to accept the terms of the offer. No contract would be created because the offer was automatically terminated upon the death of Jones.

Acceptance. An acceptance is the manifestation of agreement to the terms of the offer. This consent can be accomplished by word or deed. For example, if the offer was "I promise to pay you $200 if you promise to paint my house," the acceptance is made by promising to paint the house. The contract comes into existence at the time the *promise to paint* the house is made. On the other hand, if the offer was "I promise to pay you $200 if you paint my house," the acceptance is made by the actual painting of the house. The contract comes into existence at the time the house is actually painted. These examples illustrate the principle that the means of acceptance is conditioned by the terms of the offer. Since the offeror will be legally bound by a contract, this rule permits him to name the conditions under which he will contract. Any other rule would permit the offeree to change the terms of the contract without the offeror's consent to additional or different terms.

Another important rule of contract law prevents a person from accepting the terms of an offer if he is not aware of its existence. The classic example of this rule is the "Wanted Poster," advertising a bounty for the return of a fugitive from justice. If the person who returns the outlaw is unaware of the reward, he cannot legally accept the offer. In other words, he cannot create an enforceable contract to have the reward money paid to him.

> Dodge City Coach Lines offers $500 for the return of John Bart. Tex Williams, unaware of the reward poster, captures Bart and returns him to justice. Since Williams is unaware of the reward offer, no contract is created. If Dodge City Coach Lines refuses to pay, Williams cannot recover in a lawsuit brought to enforce payment of the reward.
>
> On the other hand, if Williams is aware of the reward and returned Bart to justice with the reward money in mind, a valid contract has been created. If Coach Lines refuses to pay the reward money voluntarily, Williams can take them to court and force them to pay.

Another special rule regulating the acceptance of contracts stems from our heavy dependence on modern methods of communications. The acceptance of the offer is valid at the time the assent is deposited for communication, not when the assent is actually communicated to the offeror. For example:

> Baker writes Carroll and offers to pay fifty-seven cents per carton of shotgun shells. Two days later, Carroll sends a letter to Baker in which he agrees to sell him the shells at that price. The contract comes into existence at the time the letter of acceptance is deposited in the mailbox. There is no requirement that the acceptance be received by the offeror (Baker) before a contract comes into existence.

Another important rule to remember is that silence, by itself, never constitutes acceptance of a contract. A person cannot create a contract by making the following offer: "I promise to sell you membership in the ABC Book Club. If you desire to join, do nothing, and you will automatically be enrolled." In this situation, the recipient's silence would not create a contract. A person making an offer to contract cannot unilaterally impose upon the offeree the duty to reply in order to reject the offer. This is an important rule to remember when dealing with slick-selling artists who are attempting to impose a contractual obligation upon you.

Consideration. This is often a confusing term. Lawyers define it as the act or forbearance from an act that constitutes the inducement for the contracting party to enter into a contract. Since a contract is essentially a promise, something should be given in return to hold the promisor to his promise. That which is given in return is called "consideration." The following examples illustrate what is meant by this term.

> Thomas says to Jones: "I promise to pay you $200 if you fix my car." If Jones fixes the car, a valid contract is created and Thomas will be held to the terms of his promise. In this case, the *act* of fixing the car constitutes the "consideration."

> Thomas says to Jones: "I promise to pay you $200 if you promise to fix my car." If Jones promises to fix the car, there is a valid contract and Thomas will be held to the terms of his promise. Jones's promise binds Thomas to the terms. Thus, Jones's promise is the "consideration" for the contract.

Notice that consideration can be a promise or an act. It can also be a forbearance from acting, as in the following example:

> Thomas says to Jones: "I promise to pay you $200 if you do not build a 'grudge wall' between our respective properties for the next two years." If dur-

> ing that period Jones refrains from building the wall, a valid contract will be created and Thomas will be held to the terms of his promise. Jones's forbearance from constructing a wall to which he is legally entitled constitutes the "consideration" for this contract.

According to the law, consideration must have two essential elements: It must have value, and it must be bargained for and given in exchange for the promise. We have already discussed several examples which demonstrate the principle of consideration. There is no contract if the act is not *bargained for,* as in those situations in which the promisor is merely asking the other person to do what that person already must do. Suppose Powell promises Roberts $100 if Roberts "tells the truth" at a trial in which Roberts is a witness for Powell. This would be an unenforceable agreement because it lacks consideration. Since everyone has a duty to tell the truth, Roberts would not be doing any act for which Powell has bargained.

Because no consideration is present, there is no contract when Alice's grandfather tells her: "I promise to give you $1,000." This is a bare promise. Alice does not have to promise anything, do anything, or refrain from doing anything. Therefore, since nothing is to be given in return for the grandfather's promise, there is no enforceable contract.

The other requirement is that the consideration have some value. It does not have to be a fair bargain, however, since the law guarantees a person's right to contract to whatever terms he desires. If the interested parties agree to the terms, the law is not permitted to rewrite or negate the intentions of the contractors in an attempt to make a "fair" contract.

Most people are aware that many contracts which they sign contain a phrase "in consideration of $1.00 and other valuable considerations." Normally, the law will uphold contracts where one dollar is the consideration—no matter what it is exchanged for. This is based on the theory that one dollar has some value. Although it may not be a fair exchange, the law will not ordinarily inquire into the "fairness" of the contract. An exception to this law is in the exchange of fixed values.

> Jones promises to pay Williams $200 if Williams promises to pay Jones $1.00. In this case, the exchange is inadequate on the face of the agreement. Therefore, the law will not enforce this contract.

This area of "consideration" is one of the most confusing aspects of the law of contracts since there are many exceptions and additions to the simple principles which have been outlined above. Once a person is familiar with these principles, he will be able to recognize a problem in this area when one arises in his personal or business affairs. Once the problem is recognized, he can secure competent legal advice for its final resolution.

Types of contracts

There are many types of contracts. They can be written or oral, express or implied, valid, void or voidable. Some contracts include several types. For example, there can be a voidable express contract.

Written and oral. The old saying that it has to be in writing to be of any legal value had its origin in the Statute of Frauds. The rule was first enacted in England, later adopted in the United States, and still later partially modified by the Uniform Commercial Code which is now in effect in every state but Louisiana.

Many people believe that an oral agreement is not valid. On the contrary, most oral contracts are valid and fully enforceable. Their sole disadvantage is that they are more difficult to prove. The only contracts which must be in writing are those specifically enumerated by the law.

Thus, the following contracts must be written:

- A contract for the sale of land or for the transfer of an interest in land; for example, a lease of land for more than one year.

• Any contract that is not to be performed within one year of the making of the contract. For example, "A" and "B" contract that "B" shall store "A's" property for two years. This contract can be fully performed only in two years; it cannot be performed within one year.

• A contract to guarantee the payment of a debt. Able owes Baker $200, but he refuses to pay. Baker is prepared to sue Able for the money. Crow (Able's good friend) visits Baker and asks him not to sue Able. Crow says that if Able does not pay the debt within one month, then he (Crow) will pay it. This is a valid contract, but it must be in writing to be enforceable.

• Any contract made by an executor or administrator of an estate in which he promises to pay a debt of the deceased with his own money is subject to the Statute of Frauds. This contract must be in writing in order to be legally enforceable.

• A contract for the sale of goods for the price of $500 or more must be in writing. Also it must be signed by the person against whom the enforcement is made. For instance, Andrews buys a sailboat from Donaldson's Boat Sales for $2,000. This contract must be in writing. If Donaldson hopes to recover in the event that Andrews does not pay the full purchase price, he must be sure that Andrews has signed a written contract.

The Statute of Frauds has spawned an enormous amount of litigation involving both the applicability of the law to specific situations and the legitimacy of particular types of written contracts. Courts often regard the Statute as a necessary evil and attempt to bypass it if possible. By doing so, the court gives legal effect to the parties' agreement or contract.

Formal contract. This type of contract essentially has been bypassed by the modernization of law and commerce. Its basis was the promisor's seal imprinted on wax. These contracts were called formal because of the great solemnity or formality which traditionally attended the attaching of a man's seal to the document. Today, most states have abolished the legal efficacy of formal contracts. However, if the contract is subject to the Statute of Frauds, it still must be in writing.

Express and implied contracts. In an express contract the terms of the contracting parties' promises are clearly outlined. Each side states what he will do. For example, "A" agrees to pay "B" twenty dollars if "B" caters a dinner party. An implied contract is one in which the terms are filled in by the conduct of the parties. Thus a person who goes to a dentist implies that he promises to pay for the work, although there is no express mention of fees or any other terms. It is important to remember that there is no difference in the legal efficacy of express contracts and contracts implied in fact.

Unilateral and bilateral. There is no difference in the legal effect of a unilateral or a bilateral contract. It is the content that differentiates the two. In a unilateral contract, the promise of one person is given in exchange for an *act* of the other person. Jones promises to pay Smith if Smith *paints* Jones's house. States differ on whether there is a legally binding contract before the house is painted.

In a bilateral contract the promise of one person is given in exchange for the *promise* of the other person. Jones promises to pay Smith if Smith *promises* to paint Jones's house. The legally binding obligation arises as soon as the promise to paint is made, not when the house is actually painted. The difference between these two contracts is very important in the conduct of one's daily affairs. Important legal questions are determined by whether there is an actual creation of a contract. The existence of the contract will be determined by the terms of the promise and whether the act or promise was actually made.

Void, voidable, and valid. A void contract is one which the law will not uphold. In fact, in the eyes of the law, the "contract" does not exist. Neither party to the contract can change this. A "voidable" contract is valid, but its validity can be avoided by one of the parties to the contract.

Voidable contracts include those of infants, minors, drunks, or insane persons.

Valid contracts are those which contain all the essential elements of a contract: offer, acceptance, legally capable parties, and consideration. Not all valid contracts are enforceable in a court of law, however. Contracts which are required to be in writing under the Statute of Frauds are still valid even if they are not written. The Statute of Frauds merely provides that no legal action can be taken upon that type of contract if it is not written.

Executory and executed. These terms refer to the time relative to the completion of the contract. A contract in which the respective acts have not yet been performed is called an executory contract. Once the acts have been completed, it is referred to as an executed contract.

> Baker promises to landscape Carr's home. Carr promises to pay Baker when the work is completed. At this point, there is an executory contract, fully enforceable in a court of law. Once Baker landscapes the home and Carr pays him the agreed-upon price, the respective performances have been accomplished and the contract has been executed. At this point there is no need for enforcement, because the contract has already been performed.

The importance in knowing the different types of contracts lies not in their intrinsic worth; rather, it lies in the fact that a person who is untrained in the law can use a basic knowledge of contract principles to recognize a legal problem when he is confronted by one. With the information in this chapter, he can also avoid legal problems by utilizing, beforehand, the rules of contracts.

Interpretation of contracts

Contracts are not always clear-cut. Disputes may arise as to a contract's meaning or its terms of enforcement. Sometimes these arguments result in attempts to have the contract enforced in court. The purpose of any contract litigation is to interpret what the parties originally put in writing. To provide uniform guidelines for interpretation, the law has developed many rules for courts and lawyers to follow.

One of these rules is the "Parol Evidence Rule." In contract law, "parol" refers to oral and written statements. Thus, if two persons have signed a written contract and intended it to express the full terms of their agreement, no court, in interpreting that contract, will admit as evidence any written or oral statements made prior to the signing of the written contract. Thus, a person cannot contradict or vary the terms of a written contract by introducing for the court's consideration evidence of discussions that occurred before the written agreement was signed.

> Johnson goes to Ace Auto Sales to buy a car. After finding a car he likes, he and the salesman negotiate an oral contract. Part of their presale discussion concerns Johnson's desire to remove the radio from the old car that he is trading in. Believing in the salesman's good faith, Johnson signs the sales agreement, although it does not mention the radio. When it is time for the actual transfer, the auto company refuses to let him remove the radio. Consequently, the deal falls through. Sometime later, in a suit brought over the contract, Johnson attempts to convince the court that he should have been permitted to take out the radio prior to the actual trade-in. Since no mention of this discussion was made in the contract, the court will not permit this parol evidence to be considered in interpreting the contract's meaning.

There are exceptions to the parol evidence rule. The law allows the introduction of parol evidence if there is some indication that a purported contract is the result of fraud, duress, or illegality. In any of these circumstances a binding contract does not exist. Secondly, parol evidence is admissible to show that the written agreement does not include all the terms of the contract. The third exception arises when the terms of a contract are vague or ambiguous. In this case oral evidence can be introduced to help clarify the meaning of the contract. For example, it may include the term "barrel." In the oil industry, a barrel means forty gallons. However, in the beer industry, a barrel refers to thirty gallons. In this situation oral evidence would be permitted to explain the usage of the term in the contract.

Other rules of interpretation state that words be given their plain and usual meaning, except when customary business usage indicates a special meaning, or when a technical word is defined. Obvious mistakes of grammar or punctuation are corrected by the courts. However, ambiguous words will generally be construed more unfavorably against the party who used them. If there is a conflict between a printed word and a written word, the written word will govern. So also, when there is a conflict between a figure numeral and a written numeral, the written version will prevail.

Although they may seem unyielding, the purpose of these rules is to help the court interpret the contract in a manner that best expresses the intent of those who made it.

Breach of contract

A contract is not usually taken to court unless one of the parties has refused to honor its terms or has performed only part of his obligation. Appropriately, this area of law is known as breach of contract law. Legally it is defined as the unjustified failure to perform any part or all of what was promised in the contract. To compensate for this failure, the injured party is entitled to relief from the courts.

A breach of contract can be *entire* or *partial.* If entire, the injured person is entitled to recover in money damages the value of the contract.

For example:

> XYZ Construction Company agrees to build an addition to Jones's home for $3,000 and to build it by

June 1, 1971. The construction company, on June 1, 1971, has not started construction and indicates that it will not start construction. This is a total breach of the contract by XYZ Construction Company. Jones will be able to sue the company for the damages he suffered due to their nonperformance.

That is an example of total breach. If the contract is not carried out entirely or is performed defectively, the result is a partial breach of contract. The injured party is entitled to a partial recovery dependent on the portion of the contract that has actually been completed.

XYZ Construction Company agrees to build an addition to Jones's home at a cost of $3,000 and to have it completed by June 1, 1971. The construction is ostensibly completed on June 1, 1971; but, on inspection, Jones discovers that a number of the bricks used in the addition are crumbling. This action results in a partial breach of contract. Because the contract was substantially fulfilled, the terms of the contract will be enforced. However, because of the slight defect in the company's performance of the contract, Jones is entitled to that portion of money which represents compensation for the use of defective materials.

Remedies for breach of contract

In contract law, an injured party is generally entitled to two different remedies: damages or specific performance.

Damages. Damages means money. It is the sum of money awarded to the injured party as a compensation for the losses he sustained due to a breach of contract. This sum is called the *measure of damages.* The court measures the damages in an attempt to put the injured party in as good a position as he would have been had the other person fulfilled his obligations under the contract.

Acme Retail Store enters into a contract by which Ace Manufacturing Company will sell it 10,000

> items for $.60 per item—a total cost of $6,000. Thereafter, the seller, Ace, repudiates the entire contract, refusing to perform at all. Since Acme needs the items, it is forced to go to Trans-Limited Manufacturing Company to buy the same goods. However, the market forces Acme to pay $.80 per item, or a total cost of $8,000. When Acme sues Ace, it is entitled to damages equal to the extra amount it paid when forced to make a new contract. Thus, if the first contract had been fully executed, Acme would have spent $6,000 to purchase 10,000 items. Because of the breach, it was forced to spend $8,000. Therefore, the damages which Acme suffered would amount to $2,000 ($8,000 less $6,000 = $2,000). In court, the company would be entitled to recover that amount of money.

According to the law, any breach, no matter how insignificant, gives the injured person a right to recover. This is true even when there are no actual damages. Suppose, in our earlier example, that Acme could have bought the same items elsewhere for $.60 per item. The firm would have suffered no actual loss of money, but it would still be permitted to recover "nominal" damages. In this example, the court would perhaps award a recovery amount of "$1.00 and costs."

Specific performance. Specific performance consists of a court order commanding the party who violated the contract to carry out its terms. This extraordinary remedy is applied only when an award of money is insufficient to compensate the injured party for his loss.

> Harris contracts to sell Smith a valuable ten acres of land overlooking a river valley. After the contract is signed, Harris suddenly decides that he does not want to sell the land. Smith takes Harris to court and asks the court to order Harris to sell the land to him; in other words to specifically perform the terms of the contract. Because land is unique—Smith cannot buy that land anywhere else—and

> because a sum of money is inadequate to validly compensate him for the loss of the land, the court will order Harris to sell the land to Smith.

This is an extremely powerful remedy, and courts have sometimes been reluctant to grant the request for specific performance. Consequently, they have restricted its use to those situations in which a sum of money cannot adequately compensate the injured person for not having the contract performed. Normally, the subject matter of the contract is unique, such as, land, valuable paintings, or antiques.

Law of agency

Many contracts are created, executed, or terminated through the use of an agent. Real estate agents, rental agents, insurance brokers—even gas station attendants are classified as agents.

Agency is essentially a relationship created by law in which one person, the principal, grants a second person, the agent, the power to act on his behalf. For example, Jones hires Smith to handle his investments. Jones has given Smith the power to buy and sell stocks and bonds in Jones' name. Although Smith executes the order to buy 100 shares of General Motors stock, it is Jones who is legally responsible for the purchase price. As an agent, Smith is not liable for the money.

Types of agents. The authority of an agent ranges from a narrow and defined duty to a broad power of action. A *general agent* has the authority to handle a wide range of activities or to conduct a series of transactions. A developer, Acme Real Estate, hires Brown to promote the sale of the subdivision. Brown is a general agent. A *special agent* has a limited grant of authority. He is generally hired to handle a specific transaction. For example, White names Baker as his agent for the sole purpose of selling his lawn mower. Baker is a special agent. A *subagent* is employed by the agent to aid him in performing his job. If Baker hires Able to help him sell the lawn mower, Able is a subagent. An *apparent agent,* or an agent with apparent authority, is one who, through his own actions or those of the principal, leads a third person to reasonably believe that he has the authority to act for the principal. For example, White gives Casey the title to his automobile, but gives him no authority to sell the car. Casey approaches Black and offers to sell him the automobile. Seeing the title in Casey's hand, Black reasonably concludes that Casey is White's agent and therefore possesses the authority to sell the car. Casey is an agent with apparent authority.

Principals. There are also different types of principals: disclosed, undisclosed, and partially disclosed. If the agent is allowed to disclose the identity of the person for whom he is acting, he is working for a *disclosed principal.* The principal is *undisclosed* if the third party is unaware that the agent is an agent. In other words, he does not know that the agent is actually representing another individual. If the third person knows that he is dealing with an agent but does not know the identity of the principal, he is confronted with the situation of the *partially disclosed principal.*

Power of attorney. A formally executed legal document granting an individual the power to act "generally" or for some specifically limited purpose is known as a power of attorney. For example, an individual might grant another individual a power of attorney to register his car in another state, to sign a lease, or to sell a house. A written power of attorney is usually prepared when the third party is either unfamiliar with the agent or cannot, by law or custom, accept the agent's word that he has been granted this authority by the principal. A power of attorney is terminated upon the death of the principal, on the date specified in the document, or upon the revocation of the power. In the latter case, all copies of the document must be destroyed.

Responsibilities of agent and principal. An agent's responsibilities include the following obligations:

- He must use reasonable care in performing his duties.
- He must inform the principal of all information that is relevant to the transaction.
- He must act solely for the principal and not for his own interests.
- He cannot act beyond the scope of his authority.
- He must render a full accounting of his actions.

In return, the principal owes the agent a reasonable or agreed-upon compensation for his services. In addition, if the principal wrongfully terminates the agency, he is liable to the agent for breach of contract.

Termination of agency. An agency is generally terminated in the same manner as a power of attorney. It can be ended by a pre-expressed agreement or by mutual consent. It is also terminated by the death of either the principal or the agent or by the destruction of the subject matter of the agency. To illustrate the latter case, suppose Baker was authorized to sell Able's race horse. Before the sale was completed, the horse fell ill and died. The death of the horse—the subject matter of the agency relationship—terminated the agency agreement.

If applied with full knowledge of their implications, the concepts of agency can be particularly helpful in the execution of some contracts.

Points to remember

The essential principles of contract law have been discussed in this chapter. Because the law varies widely from state to state and because each factual situation may mean different exceptions or extensions of the principles discussed here, competent legal advice may be necessary to fully protect your interests. The contract principles can be of important use to everyone, however. A knowledge of the rules discussed in this chapter will enable a person to recognize a contract that may present a problem, especially if one does not read it thoroughly. Many people avoid this necessity by saying that the print is too small or that it is not worth the trouble. Later they discover that preventive law is the best law—ALWAYS READ THE TERMS OF THE CONTRACT.

If you have a serious question about a provision, take it to an attorney for his examination. The fee for his services may be small in comparison to the cost of not being sure that your interests are fully protected and that the terms of the contract provide what you wish them to provide. Unfortunately, many contracts are written, signed and broken before an attorney examines the terms for his client. The individual can best safeguard his interests by utilizing the principles given in this chapter to recognize specific problems arising in his everyday contractual situations and then requesting his attorney's advice on these problems.

Chapter Five

When Consumers Are Duped

There are few experiences as frustrating as being deceived by a sale or gimmick. After thoughtful reflection, an individual decides that he has been duped by a sales or advertising scheme which deceived him into signing on the dotted line. What can he do about it? Unfortunately, in most instances, nothing. Signing on the line completed a contract which will be upheld unless the individual can prove fraud. Furthermore, many deceptive practices are "illegal" only in the sense that they violate state or federal standards. These violations can be enforced by state agencies or the Federal Trade Commission, but not by individuals.

Consequently, one of the most important developments in this area is the education of the consumer. If the individual does not recognize a deceptive scheme at the time it is being perpetrated, he can do little to avoid its unfair results. On the other hand, preventive education can enable him to take economic and legal action against disreputable business practices. The individual can combat deceptive practices economically by learning to recognize deceptive schemes and thereby refusing to purchase falsely advertised goods. Preventive education also will enable the consumer to combat these practices legally. Occasionally, he will be able to institute legal action against them. However, in most instances he should report the practice to proper agencies, bureaus, and authorities. A description of deceptive schemes and advertising practices will enable the individual to recognize problems in time to avoid them.

Problems

Bait and switch. In this advertising scheme, the seller offers an item at a very low price. In other words, he baits the customer. Then, instead of encouraging the purchase of that item, the salesman "switches" the customer to a higher priced article in the line. At the same time he disparages the advertised item so that the customer will not want to buy it. Usually, the seller has few or no advertised items in stock. In other words, he has no intention of selling items at the low advertised price. This practice is often employed to sell used cars, sewing machines, vacuum cleaners, home appliances, radios, television sets, and pianos. In one instance, the seller purchased classified ads daily to promote the following item:

> Repossessed Automatic Zig–Zag Sewing Machine Cabinet model, 5 mo. old. Sews on buttons, makes buttonholes and fancy stitches. No attachments needed.
>
> UNPAID BALANCE $49.50 or take over low monthly payments of $5 per mo. Call Home Credit Dept. 333–7400

Despite these advertisements, the company had no supply of repossessed new machines. The sole purpose of the ad was to obtain customer leads. The salesmen then showed prospective buyers sewing machines that were in such poor condition as to be unusable or undesirable. At the same time, they disparaged the advertised product to discourage its purchase. Instead, they attempted and frequently managed to sell more highly priced sewing machines. In some instances, if the customer persisted in trying to buy the advertised model, the salesman refused, claiming that the item was sold out or that additional attachments had to be purchased.

It is important to note, however, that it is perfectly legal to "trade-up." Sometimes there is a fine line between a "bait and switch" and a "trade-up." It is a legitimate trade-up if the advertiser has a sufficient supply of the advertised items on stock and offers to sell them willingly. While the salesman may praise the advantages of the more expensive model, he does not disparage the qualities of the lower-priced advertised item. Under these circumstances, trading-up by the salesman is a legitimate practice. However, when the salesman refuses to sell the advertised model, when he disparages it, and when the supply of that model is insufficient to meet the normal customer demand, the seller has engaged in a "bait and switch" practice. If a situation appears to be somewhere in between these two categories, it is best to consult a legal counsel who is versed in this area of the law.

Unsolicited merchandise. In order to force the sale of merchandise, a company sometimes mails unsolicited goods to a person's home. In this way, the firm tries to force the individual to pay for the merchandise or to return it at his own expense. To halt this practice, a federal law was passed. This law allows the recipients of unwanted goods to keep them, use them, or dispose of the items in any way they see fit. Furthermore, the seller is prohibited from mailing the individual an invoice for the merchandise.

However, there are certain exceptions to this rule. Free samples may be sent to the individual if conspicuously marked as such. A charitable organization may send out address labels, decorative stamps, or similar articles as a solicitation for a donation. The individual, however, is not obligated to pay or to return the items. The final exception arises from an agreement that provides for the periodic shipment of specified merchandise, as in book and record clubs.

Deceptive pricing. This method of deceptive advertising

leads the customer to believe that he is buying an item for substantially less than its customary retail price. One form of deceptive pricing is the use of a "fictitious former price." For example, Ace Drug Store is a retailer for a small portable radio which it normally purchases wholesale for ten dollars. The usual markup is 50 percent which brings the price of the radio to fifteen dollars. However, for the first week, Ace Drug Store offers the radio for twenty dollars, although the manager knows that he will sell few, if any, at that price. The next week, he offers an "unusual bargain": "Radios 25 percent off regular price—was $20.00, now only $14.95." This advertised "bargain" is nothing of the sort. The store is using an inflated, fictitious former price. Since Ace Drug did not sell a reasonable number of radios for twenty dollars apiece, the above advertisement is a false claim. It violates the guidelines established by the Federal Trade Commission.

Another form of deceptive pricing involves the use of the term "wholesale." Occasionally, a mail order house will advertise merchandise for "wholesale" prices that are substantially higher than the usual wholesale price and sometimes more than the retail price. For example, a catalog might advertise watches as follows:

> No. 1457WWX1295 .... $23.95
> Your cost is part of our coded stock number.
> Point off two decimal points.
> (Your cost would be $12.95.)

The use of that selling technique is available only to bona fide wholesalers selling to bona fide retail trades. If the prices quoted by the "wholesaler" are fictitious, he is running the risk of being investigated and subjected to legal proceedings by the Federal Trade Commission.

Many retailers quote the suggested manufacturer's price for an article and then give their price which is often much lower. This practice is a form of deceptive advertising if the retailer claims that his price is substantially less than the normal retail price when it is not. For example, suppose the suggested retail price of a fountain pen is ten dollars, and that is the price at which it is customarily sold. Then, if ABC Retailer advertises it as "Retail $10.00—Now Only $7.50" he is promoting a legitimate reduction in the sales price. However, if the suggested manufacturer's price is ten dollars, but the pen is generally sold for seven dollars and fifty cents, the retailer would be pricing the item deceptively if he advertised "Retail $10.00—Now only $7.50."

As the reader can readily determine, the line between a legitimate price reduction and a deceptive illusion of reduction is sometimes difficult to draw. The smart consumer is best advised to shop around and compare prices, advertisements, and claims in the entire area. If he is then convinced that the pricing of an item is deceptive he should file complaints with the proper authorities. These include the stores, the Better Business Bureaus, the Federal Trade Commission, and other agencies.

Door-to-door sales. Every consumer has had his share of door-to-door salesmen offering him the once-in-a-lifetime chance to take advantage of a unique bargain. The individual who is approached by the door-to-door salesman has one problem in particular. He is unable to compare prices among similar items.

For example, one encyclopedia company employed door-to-door salesmen who claimed to be making a marketing survey. Upon entry the salesman would tell the homeowner that he was one of a select group of customers chosen to take part in a unique promotional campaign. The salesman then claimed that he was selling the encyclopedia to this select group for substantially less than the normal retail price. A state court ordered the company to stop this practice. In addition, the court allowed customers who were duped by these deceptive pricing and advertising schemes to cancel their purchases. The company was forced to refund their money.

Another notorious door-to-door sales practice is sometimes used to promote the purchases of magazine subscriptions. In one instance, a salesgirl who claimed to be earning her way through college by selling magazines solicited a two-year subscription to a nationally known magazine for twelve dollars. The customer gave the salesgirl a twelve dollar check for the two-year subscription and received a receipt marked "Paid in Full." Two weeks later the customer received a "Duplicate Office Record," an identically numbered carbon copy receipt. This carbon copy indicated that the customer had purchased a four-year subscription and that he owed additional money to the magazine subscription agency. Fortunately, a carefully written letter from an attorney resolved the situation. This practice was a blatant violation of the code of ethics of the magazine publishers' association.

As a result of its investigation of unfair door-to-door sales practices, the Federal Trade Commission ordered many companies to give customers a decision period. During this time, the individual can determine whether he really wishes to buy the merchandise or subscribe to the service. Under these FTC orders, specified companies must:

- Tell all purchasers that they have three days in which to cancel the order
- Provide blank cancellation forms which the buyer can complete and return
- Not transfer any instrument of debt to a financial institution before the expiration of five days from the date of the sale

These governmental requirements provide the customer with a weapon that can be used to neutralize the selling pressure of insistent salesmen or to fight back after an unfair sale has been initially completed.

Improper collection tactics. Many unscrupulous firms use false representation to force slow-paying customers to pay their debts. Some unethical companies send out letters that appear to be from credit bureaus or legitimate collection agencies. These letters lead the customer to believe that his bill has been turned over to a collection agency or credit bureau. Actually, the company claiming payment still possesses the bill.

Some companies send documents that appear to be legal forms. These convey the impression that a lawsuit has been instituted against the debtor for payment of the amount due. Other companies demand improper "late charges" or threaten legal action when it is actually against company policy to institute litigation against slow-paying customers. Many customers are intimidated by letters which "appear" to be from a governmental agency or court.

In one case a United States Court of Appeals upheld a Federal Trade Commission ruling that a certain company was using improper collection techniques. The company was sending payment demand notices that appeared to be from a government agency in Washington, D.C. A Los Angeles company printed and sold forms to creditors. The creditor will fill in the debtor's name and address and return the form to the company's branch office in Washington, D.C. The Washington branch office would then mail the payment demand notice directly to the customer.

For example, John Jones agreed to buy a sewing machine from National Sewing Machine Company for $250. After three months, Jones stopped his payments on the machine. In an effort to collect the money, National Sewing Machine Company subscribed to a Los Angeles commercial form "payment demand" service. The Los Angeles company sent the "payment demand" notice to the National Sewing Machine Company which filled in John Jones' name and sent the card to its branch office in Washington, D.C. The form was then mailed to John Jones from Washington, D.C., in a brown window envelope. Stamped on the envelope were two statements: "The form enclosed is Confidential. No One Else May Open," and "Postmaster: After 4 Days Return to 2823 Washington Bldg., Washington, D.C." The "payment demand" form was similar to the following:

> You have 10 days to pay the amount of $________ on the claim of . . . . You are scheduled to appear in the CREDITOR'S OFFICE, located at ________

> in the city of ____________ State of ____________
> on or before two o'clock in the afternoon of the
> __________ day of ______________ 19____ to pay
> the balance requested or give satisfactory reasons
> in PERSON why the AMOUNT has not been paid.
> IF MAILING PAYMENT TO CREDITOR REFER TO
> FILE NO. ____________.

On this same form, in a box were printed the words:

> "THIS DEMAND IS MADE TO GIVE YOU A LAST OPPORTUNITY TO PAY BEFORE ACTION IS TAKEN ON SAID CLAIM."

In many cases, this form notice led the customer to believe that a government agency was applying pressure to force his payment of the debt. However, no government pressure was being applied. If the customer did not pay, the company would send another notice. The "payment demand" would arrive in a brown window envelope stamped "Washington, D.C." This "payment demand" form would state:

> Subject to the Law of the State of ______________.
> A Creditor may request an Attorney-at-Law to attach after Judgment Property such as Automobile, Jewelry, Boat, Live Stock, Crops, Machinery, House, Real Estate, Bank Account, Bank Vault, Stocks, Bonds, and Earning, Commission, or Salary.

The Federal Trade Commission found, and the U.S. Court agreed, that the repetition of the words "Washington, D.C.," the use of elaborate type styles simulating legal documents, and the overall format of the procedure, tended to exploit the assumption of many debtors that anything coming from Washington, D.C., comes from the government. The FTC and the court ordered a halt to this misrepresentation.

By learning to recognize misrepresentation and other improper procedures, the individual can help curb illegal practices and protect his own financial interests. Once he knows that it is illegal, the individual can no longer be intimidated by such treatment. His best course of action is to notify his attorney, the Better Business Bureau, the Federal Trade Commission and any other consumer agencies.

Legal Remedies

The legal remedies available to a consumer who has been duped by deceptive advertising are not always as effective as could be desired. An individual buyer, a state agency, a credit or better business bureau, and the Federal Trade Commission can all exercise economic and legal pressure against companies that use deceptive practices to misrepresent their products. However, the result achieved by each party's action can differ widely.

Individual. The consumer's main course of legal action against a merchant or company that has deceived him is to sue for fraud. However there are two difficulties inherent in this approach:

- The cost of the litigation
- The difficulty of proving the case

In most instances of purchase resulting from deceptive pricing or advertising, the total amount involved ranges between \$100 and \$500. The cost of litigation can easily exceed this amount. Consequently, most individuals are willing to "chalk it up to experience." They grudgingly pay the money or agree to let the merchant repossess the item for failure to make proper payments. Unfortunately, the unethical merchant is aware that to most consumers a lawsuit is not worth the cost. As a result, many continue their misrepresentations on the theory that the risk is worth the gamble. In their opinion, the money they gain through these schemes is definitely worth the risk of being subjected to an occasional lawsuit for fraud.

The second factor weakening the individual's chance for a legal remedy is that, in most instances, his *only* course of action is to sue the seller for fraud or, as it is technically named, deceit. Furthermore, the law imposes strict requirements on the individual who is suing for deceit. In order to win his case, the plaintiff must prove five elements:

- That the seller made a false representation of a statement of fact
- That the seller knew it was false at the time the statement was made
- That the seller intended for the prospective buyer to rely on this false statement in making the purchase
- That the buyer was reasonable in relying on that statement in making his purchase
- That the buyer suffered damages because he relied on that false statement in making a purchase

Proving these elements in connection with deceptive advertising and sales schemes is often difficult.

For example, suppose National Sewing Machine Company falsely informs John Jones that machine X-20v is new and that it sews forward, backward, and zig-zag. Jones relies on those representations in purchasing the machine. He will be able to recover for fraud if he can prove also that the company *knew* the statements were false, that the company gave him false information to induce the purchase of the machine, and that he was reasonable in relying on that information in making his purchase. However, if the individual fails to prove any one of these elements, his case will be dismissed. In many cases, it is almost impossible to prove conclusively that all five elements existed.

State agencies. Unfortunately, few states have enough strict consumer protection laws. Furthermore, those states that have good laws frequently lack the personnel to enforce them. As a result, many consumers have had little real protection at the state level. However, as consumer concern sweeps the country, many states have begun to review the problems created by deceptive schemes and the legal remedies available to combat their use.

The Maryland legislature, for example, has passed a bill outlawing the "you were selected" prize schemes. This practice consists of sending out letters to individuals informing them that they have won a prize. When the individual comes to collect his "free gift," the salesman gives him a hard sales pitch. The Maryland law would make it unlawful practice to notify any person "as part of an advertising scheme that he has won a prize, received an award, or has been selected or is eligible to receive anything of value, which is conditioned upon his purchasing any item or submitting to a sales promotion effort."

To the extent that states continue to update their consumer protection laws and provide adequate personnel to enforce the laws' provisions, the welfare of the state's residents will be more fully protected and the number of successful schemes will be reduced.

Federal Trade Commission. The Federal Trade Commission was established in 1914 in an attempt to limit unfair methods of competition. It now uses its authority to stop unfair or deceptive acts and practices in the commercial world. For instance, if someone reports that a company engages in unfair or deceptive practices, the Federal Trade Commission has the power and the authority to investigate the matter. However, the FTC can only investigate practices which are "in the public interest." In other words it cannot and will not intervene into a purely private controversy. The alleged deceptive practice must be part of the company's general course of business. If the Federal Trade Commission discovers that the company has engaged in deceptive practices it will issue a "cease and desist" order against the company. In effect, this is a government order demanding that the company stop using practices which the FTC has declared unfair. If the company violates this order, the Commission can sue the company in a federal court and collect as much as $5,000 for each violation.

Consumer class actions. The consumer class action, which was discussed but not passed during the 91st Congress, could provide a new method for individual consumers to seek legal remedies against companies who have sold them merchandise or services through the use of fraudulent practices. In law, a "class action" permits several individuals to join together in a "class" and jointly bring an action against the defendant. This permits the individuals to share the costs of litigation.

For example, John Jones believed that a sewing machine company had sold him a very expensive sewing machine ($450) illegally. If he wished to bring an individual legal action against the company, the costs of the lawsuit might exceed $2,500. But, suppose John Jones found twenty-four other individuals who also believed that the sewing machine company had used fraudulent means to sell them merchandise. If they decided to take a class action, the costs per individual would be small. Thus, if this trial also cost $2,500, the cost per individual would be $100 ($2,500 divided by 25).

As can be seen, a consumer class action would compensate for the individual consumer's inability to litigate small individual losses. It would enable one or more representatives of a group of consumers with similar injuries to place a group injury before a court.

How to cope with deceptive advertising or sales schemes. What can the individual citizen do about salesmen who make their living by deceiving potential customers? The consumer does not have to be a lawyer to fight back. The only requirement is that he be sufficiently informed about deceptive practices to recognize their use.

No matter what the scheme, there is one common purpose: To deceive the buyer into believing that he is getting more for his money than he could anywhere else. Unfortunately, the buyer later discovers that he has paid substantially more for the product than he expected.

The first important rule in driving out the minority of disreputable businesses, is intelligent buying on the part of the consumer. This is where the individual's knowledge of deceptive schemes proves invaluable. Recognizing deceptive practices permits the buyer to shop around and select legitimate bargains. Reputable businesses will welcome the discerning buyer who shops for the most quality for the least amount of money. Therefore, Rule No. 1 is: *Shop intelligently.*

If the buyer believes that he has been deceived, he need

not shrug it off as the price of experience. He can make his indignation known by reporting his facts and opinions to the merchant, preferably in person. If the merchant is unaware of the practice, he can correct the situation immediately. If so, the problem is solved and both the consumer and the business benefit. If the merchant ignores or refuses to satisfy a complaint, the consumer should report him to one of the community organizations whose task is to upgrade business practices. Generally, this is the Better Business Bureau. While the Bureau usually brings no legal action against the merchant, it will notify him and request that he explain the complaint. If the company wishes to maintain its reputation, it will comply with the request. The Bureau advises that any consumer complaint include copies of all correspondence with the company. In addition, the Bureau asks complainants to submit the following information:

Full name and address
Name or brief description of merchandise
Date ordered
Amount paid
Receipt, order, invoice or account number
Payment by check, money order, or cash
Whether or not you have the canceled check
The date of your last contact with the company

Many people are afraid to get involved. They will let the matter die, rather than fight back. Rule No. 2, therefore, is: *Report complaints to consumer protection organizations.*

The layman is also encouraged to report the facts about deceptive advertising schemes to the media that advertise the products. Write to the newspapers and TV or radio stations. Their good reputation depends on the truth of their advertising. If enough people complain of an advertiser's practices, the media will refuse to accept advertising copy from him. In this way, the consumer can deprive the merchant of an important means of peddling his deception. The individual can promote effective consumer protection at the small cost of his time and postage. Therefore, Rule

No. 3 is: *Report complaints to the news-media.*

A fourth method of combating disreputable companies is to report the complaint to the local law enforcement agencies, such as the county attorney or the state attorney general. Most states have some deceptive advertising laws and many are enforced vigorously. Using consumer-supplied information, the local governments can legally stamp out misrepresentation schemes and deceptive practices. Rule No. 4 is: *Consult your local government.*

The consumer can also report his problem to the Federal Trade Commission. A letter to the FTC should contain the same information that one would send to the Better Business Bureau and any additional relevant facts. The letter should be sent to:

Federal Trade Commission
Washington, D.C. 20580

The Commission has a broad responsibility to halt "unfair methods of competition in commerce and unfair or deceptive acts or practices in commerce." Unfortunately, the Commission cannot handle private controversies. It concentrates on cases having "sufficient public interest." However, the layman is advised to let the Commission determine whether his particular complaint has public interest. Many deceptive practices are more widespread than the victim realizes. Therefore, rule No. 5 is: *Write to the Federal Trade Commission.*

Thus, without spending any money except for postage, the layman can help bring to justice the relatively few merchants who insist upon using deceptive practices and advertising to sell their merchandise. To put these five rules into effect it is not necessary to consult a lawyer. However, if the complaint involves a substantial amount of money, it is perhaps best to consult a lawyer as to the advisability of taking direct legal action. Remember, it is the "consumer-educated" layman who can spot, avoid, and help curtail deceptive advertising practices.

Chapter Six

Your Rights With Your Creditors

Modern America has produced an amazing surge in the availability and use of credit. In past decades, it was a wise man who adhered to the principle that a person should pay cash for everything, except perhaps a house or car. It is still a good principle not to borrow except when necessary. However, with the advent of a modern economy, the ease of communications, the high mobility of American society, and the development of the computer, most Americans have credit available to them, and most make use of it.

Furthermore, the sellers have revolutionized their marketing to meet the demand. Today, virtually everything is available on credit, or the "Buy Now—Pay Later" plan. A consumer can use a major credit card to charge such varied items as a European vacation, college tuition, his church donation, airplane tickets, car rentals, dinner, department store items, gasoline, a Playboy party, bail if he happens to be an accused in Phoenix, and even his own funeral.

In some states, he can now charge his federal income tax. A customer may charge up to $500 in taxes if his bank accepts the method. Cardholders receive $7^1/_4$ x $3^1/_2$ inch cards, made out to the Internal Revenue Service. These are actually checks deposited by the IRS in cooperating banks and subsequently billed to the taxpayer along with his other credit purchases.

Credit traditionally has meant the sale of property in return for a promise of deferred payment. For example, Charles Customer goes to Acme Department Store to buy a television set. The store sells him the television in return for his promise to pay the entire purchase price upon receiving the bill. This usually arrives within thirty days. Thus, credit has been extended to the consumer although there is no additional charge for the privilege of deferred payment. However, if Charles wants a longer time to pay for the television he must pay for the privilege of using the set. This additional cost is "interest."

Interest is the cost of credit. If a formal contract is written for the purchase of a specific item, the credit extended is generally called an installment loan. The cost of an installment loan equals the purchase price of the item plus the cost of credit (interest) plus the cost of the paper work involved in administering the loan (a service charge).

The most common credit arrangement is the revolving charge account agreement. By its terms, the buyer, upon receipt of his bill, agrees to pay the creditor either the entire amount outstanding, in which case no interest is charged, or ten percent of the outstanding amount. In the latter case, the minimum payment is ten dollars, and a "finance charge" is added to the account.

If the store is large enough, it may operate its own credit department. If it is smaller, it may take part in a credit program directed by an independent credit institution or by an interbank operation. The major gasoline companies offer this form of credit arrangement to their customers. Another large source of credit is the nation-wide, multi-purpose credit agencies.

Due to the high standard of living in the United States and the increased availability of computerized account processing, it is relatively easy for most Americans to pay for goods and services with credit. For these Americans, the important question is: How much will credit cost me?

At one time, it was difficult to find the answer. One would routinely examine his bills, noting an apparently minor cost or "monthly handling charge of $1^1/_2$ percent on the amounts past due." The consumer accepted this amount as a nominal cost, believing that it barely paid for the creditor's bookkeeping of his account. After a while, however, he computed the cost on a yearly basis. The customer was astounded to find that he was paying an annual interest rate of 18 percent (12 months x $1^1/_2$ percent per month = 18 percent).

Due to increased public displeasure over this confusing method of stating the cost of credit, Congress passed the Consumer Credit Protection Act, generally known as the Truth in Lending Law. This statute applies to all consumer credit transactions but not to business or commercial transactions. Effective as of July 1, 1969, its main purpose is *disclosure*. The law requires creditors to reveal the exact cost of credit. This allows the consumer to compare various credit plans. Furthermore, the law requires the creditor to disclose this information in his advertising, at the time an obligation (contract or sale) is incurred, and in every bill sent to the consumer.

One major change effected by the law concerns the terms used to describe credit costs. Before the enactment of this law creditors used a variety of terms to designate the cost of credit. Examples of these nebulous terms include interest charge, monthly charge, service fee, investigation fee, administrative handling, carrying charge, and time-price differential. However, as a result of the new law, the customer finds two terms in bold black print on his monthly credit account bill: ANNUAL PERCENTAGE RATE and FINANCE CHARGE.

These two terms reveal at a glance how much the individual is paying for his credit and its relative cost in percentage terms. Instead of a confusing notation indicating a monthly carrying charge of $1^1/_2$ percent per month, there is a clear statement that the ANNUAL PERCENTAGE RATE is 18 percent. Moreover, the rest of the charges are all included in the FINANCE CHARGE. This column states the total cost paid by the consumer for the use of credit. Technically, this FINANCE CHARGE includes the following costs: interest; service charge; carrying charge; loan fee; the time-price differential; and any investigation or credit report fee. Thus, the FINANCE CHARGE can be defined as the cost of credit over the life of the loan as expressed in dollars and cents.

The rules requiring complete disclosure of FINANCE CHARGE and ANNUAL PERCENTAGE RATE apply both to open-end credit such as revolving charge accounts, gasoline credit cards and multi-purpose credit accounts, and to single transaction credit sales. Examples of single sales credit or consumer installment loan items include automobiles, washing machines, television sets, and other major appliances. An article of this type is normally sold under an agreement which must fully disclose the cash price, less any down payment or trade-in allowance, plus any other charges. This includes any FINANCE CHARGE. The final amount should show the total deferred payment price or the complete cost to the customer. There can be no hidden post-sale charges. This agreement also must indicate the total ANNUAL PERCENTAGE RATE.

To illustrate, suppose Charles Customer goes to his local TV & Appliance Store to trade in his old hi-fi for a new stereo entertainment center. He wishes to finance the sale. The store owner must furnish him with a Retail Installment Contract which clearly states that the cash price is $950; the down payment, $200; and the trade-in allowance, $250. This leaves $500 to be financed. Furthermore, the store imposes a FINANCE CHARGE of $100 over the thirty months of scheduled monthly payments. Using a special table to compute the ANNUAL PERCENTAGE RATE, the store concludes that the percentage for this sale is 14.75 percent. Consequently, Charles knows the exact rate of interest he must pay for the privilege of a deferred payment plan on his stereo unit. Moreover, he realizes how much more it costs to pay by credit than by cash ($100). He can also use the figures quoted by this merchant as a basis of comparison should he decide to go to another store. Since all merchants must express credit costs in the same terms, ANNUAL PERCENTAGE RATE and FINANCE CHARGE, Charles can compare both the cost of the competitor's stereo and the cost of his credit plan. In this way, the Truth in Lending Law fulfills its purpose. Charles is fully able to shop for the best buy.

The Truth in Lending Law also gives the consumer the means to protect himself against merchants who refuse to disclose their interest rates. Although many other laws permit only government agencies to act in the public interest, the Truth in Lending Law allows the individual consumer to bring violators to court. If the consumer can demonstrate that the merchant refused to disclose the FINANCE CHARGE, he can recover damages amounting to twice the sum of the FINANCE CHARGE, plus court costs and reasonable attorney's fees. This latter item may amount to a substantial sum. The minimum recovery is $100; the maximum is $1,000, exclusive of court costs and attorney's fees.

For example, John Jones buys a used automobile from Acme Sales Company. The contract does not mention the FINANCE CHARGE. It lists only the amount and the number of payments. Using his own computation, Jones discovers a $300 difference between the total amount he has to pay, $1,550, and the cash price of the item, $1,250. The company failed to list this $300 FINANCE CHARGE in the contract. Consequently, Jones can bring an action against Acme and recover $600 (recovery is twice the FINANCE CHARGE), plus his court costs and attorney's fees. If the court costs are $35 and his attorney's fee is $700, the total amount of damages awarded to Jones will be $1,335.

By availing themselves of this legal remedy, consumers can encourage merchants to conform to the law's requirements for disclosure. There are two limitations, however. The court action must be initiated within one year of the violation of the regulation. Normally, the date of the violation is the date the contract is signed. Secondly, the merchant's failure to disclose a charge must be intentional. An honest mistake does not carry legal liability.

Another credit controversy was resolved in October, 1970, with the passage of an amendment to the Consumer Credit Protection Act. As a result of this amendment, federal law prohibits the issuance and mailing of credit cards to individuals except upon request. Furthermore, under the provisions of the amendment, the individual is not liable for the unauthorized use of a card which he has neither requested nor received.

Thus, under existing law, the individual is only liable for the unauthorized use of a credit card bearing his name under the following circumstances:

- When he has a credit contract with a company and fails to notify it of the theft or loss of his card
- When he possesses a credit card and facilitates its unauthorized use through negligence.

Thus, federal law guarantees everyone the right to decide whether he wants credit. Moreover, the individual is entitled to full knowledge of the nature of credit. This includes the costs in terms of ANNUAL PERCENTAGE RATE (interest), and the FINANCE CHARGE for the usc of credit. As long as these objectives are fulfilled, there can be effective co-ordination between the expanding needs and desires of consumers and the economics of a computerized credit account system.

Chapter Seven

Legal Tips for Better Banking

Most Americans are in some way bound to a bank. The relationship may be in the form of a loan agreement, a mortgage, or, as is most often the case, a bank account. Establishing a bank account takes so little time that many customers fail to consider the rights and liabilities that flow from this relationship. In the same manner, writing checks as payment for goods and services is second nature to most people. But what is the individual's legal recourse if a written check is stolen or altered and, as a result, wrongfully honored? How does he protect himself from the possibility of a false appropriation of his check?

The individual can avoid many unfortunate situations by learning the legal responsibilities of both bank and customer as concerns the usual bank accounts and the endorsement of checks. In addition, it is useful to know the rules covering the negotiation of commercial paper and holder in due course. This chapter undertakes to describe the legal aspects of banking in relation to the average customer.

Accounts

Checking account. By far, the most common banking service is the checking account. The customer can use it to his best advantage by maintaining its accuracy. The checking account provides the individual with a safe, convenient method of paying his bills. If he maintains its accuracy and retains canceled checks, he has written proof of the payment of his bills.

The bank-customer relationship is essentially a contract relationship. The customer and the bank sign a prior written contract allowing the customer to deposit money in the bank and to write checks on his account. The customer must maintain sufficient funds in the account to cover his checks. In return, the bank maintains the account, provides records, and honors the customer's checks as they are returned to the bank for collection.

The legal relationship is that of a debtor-creditor: The bank is the debtor to the extent of the creditor's or customer's deposit, and conversely. When a customer deposits money in a checking account, legal title to the money passes to the bank. The bank can use the funds for its own legitimate purposes as long as it honors its commitment to pay out money in accordance with the customer's orders. This order is contained in every check. Thus when a customer writes a check, he says to the bank: Pay to the order of the named payee the amount of money indicated on the check. The bank's duty to obey this order stems from the contract on which the account is based.

A checking account may be single or joint. If the original contract of deposit is in the name of one person, that person is the only one who can write checks on the account. If the sole owner dies, the balance of the account will go to the beneficiary named in his will. If there is no will, it will be distributed according to the laws of intestate succession (see the chapter on estate planning).

A joint tenancy or joint account has more than one owner. Each can write checks on the account. If one of the joint owners dies, the other retains complete ownership and control over the checking account. The control of the checking account is determined by the original deposit contract. The provisions of one owner's will do not affect the rights to the checking account.

A thorough knowledge of the nature and implications of both the single and the joint checking account can help the individual in the management of his personal business and in the planning of his estate.

Savings account. The contract for a savings account is similar to the agreement for a checking account. The deposit contract permits the customer to put money in his account and to receive a certain rate of interest on the balance of the account. The bank has title and use of the money. However, it must credit the customer's account with the proper interest and pay the customer the requested amount if he wishes to withdraw some or all of his funds.

In most cases, the customer's account is protected from a possible bank failure. The Federal Deposit Insurance Corporation insures bank accounts for amounts up to $20,000. More than 90 percent of the commercial banks in the United States are protected under this program. If the bank should fail, the agency will pay the depositor directly for his loss or provide him with an account of equal amount at another bank. Whether the account is insured by the F.D.I.C is another factor which the customer must consider in choosing his bank and type of account. Although bank failures are few and far between today it is best to open an account that is protected by the F.D.I.C. or by some other means.

Bank transactions. In many instances, the bank or the customer initiates special processes to further the latter's interests. These situations require the application of legal principles peculiar to the bank-customer relationship. These include the stop payment order, death of the writer, wrongfully charged accounts, wrongful acceptance of forged accounts, and "stale" checks.

Stop payment orders. The contractual agreement between the bank and the customer allows the customer to stop payment on a check that he has written and delivered. To do this, he orders the bank to refuse the check when it is presented for collection. A customer may wish to stop payment for many reasons, such as possible loss of check, failure of payee to fulfill his part of the agreement, or the passage of time.

To initiate a stop payment order, the customer fills out a special bank form which includes the name of the payee, the date and number of the check, and the amount. A written stop payment order is effective and binding on the bank for six months. Thereafter it can be renewed. The customer can even institute a stop payment order over the telephone. However, an oral order is binding on the bank for only two weeks. To be effective for a longer time, it must be put in writing. In that event, the validity of the stop payment order lasts for six months from the date of the written order.

The customer cannot order a stop payment after the bank has honored the check. He is too late; the check has been fully processed. A stop payment order must be delivered in time to give the bank a reasonable opportunity to advise its personnel of the order. Otherwise, the check may be honored inadvertently. If the bank wrongfully fails to stop payment, it is liable to the customer for the damages he has suffered. Usually, this is equal to the amount of the wrongfully honored check.

Death of the writer. The legal status of a check after the death of the writer was in dispute for many years. Finally, the Uniform Commercial Code standardized the applicable rules. According to the Code, which was adopted by every state except Louisiana, the death of the writer does not render the check null and void. The bank can still honor it in good faith. Even if the bank has been notified of the individual's death, it can continue to honor his checks for ten days from the date of death. The reasons behind this rule stem from the nature of banking. The tremendous volume of a bank's business requires that it be allowed to act with some degree of freedom. Furthermore, in most cases, the decedent intended the check to be honored when he wrote it. Thus the bank is actually carrying out his order by honoring the check.

Stale checks. Another rule of law applied to banking transactions concerns stale checks. The term "stale" describes a check that is presented to the bank for collection long after it was written. Suppose John Jones writes a check on February 10, 1970, payable to the order of "Al Smith." On November 15, 1970, Smith finally endorses the check and presents it to the bank for collection. The delay of nine months between the time the check was written and the date it was submitted makes it a stale check. Under modern law, a bank is not required to honor a check that is more than six months old. However, if the bank officers reasonably believe that the writer still wants the check honored, they may do so.

Thus, it is important to endorse checks promptly and submit them for collection. Failure to do this may result in the application of the stale-check rule, costing the individual time, money, and aggravation. A knowledge of this important banking principle can help the individual stay within the protection of the law and use it to his advantage.

Wrongful dishonor. Sometimes a bank refuses to honor a check under the mistaken belief that the customer has insufficient funds or no account. For example, Jones has an account at National Savings Bank. He writes a check on that account for $75, payable to Ritz Department Store. At the time that Ritz presents the check to National Savings for collection, Jones actually has $300 in his account. However, National Savings believes that Jones has only $30 in his account. Therefore, it marks the check "Insufficient Funds" and returns it to Ritz. As a result, Ritz concludes that Jones is no longer a good credit risk and cancels his charge account. Under the legal rules applicable to commercial transactions, National Savings Bank would be liable to Jones for the damages he suffered because it wrongfully dishonored the Ritz check.

Check alterations and wrongful endorsements

In general, modern law in this area protects the bank. The specific rules are very complex and require individual professional advice. However, the general reason behind the rule favoring the bank is to give it reasonable freedom to operate smoothly amidst a multitude of transactions. At the same time, the individual customer is often in a better position to prevent possible alterations or wrongful endorsements.

Occasionally, the original amount of a check is altered by someone other than the writer. If the person who wrote the check has contributed to the ease of alteration by leaving wide spaces between the numbers, he will not be able to recover from the bank. In this situation, the bank acted reasonably in cashing the check.

Many individuals and companies use a signature stamp or some other automatic signing device. Unauthorized personnel occasionally use this device to endorse the checks and appropriate the funds. If the account owner left the stamp or signature device where an unauthorized person could find it, his negligence contributed to the wrongful honoring of the checks. Because the checks were endorsed with the automatic stamp, the bank had no reason to suspect anything improper. Thus, its action in cashing the checks was entirely reasonable. In neither of the two examples would the individual customer recover. Although the bank wrongfully honored the checks, it did so in good faith. However, if the bank were using substandard banking procedures in its check transactions, the customer would be allowed to recover.

Because the commercial laws often favor the bank, the layman is best advised to learn the applicable legal rules and to take care that his own bank transactions are not subject to the wrong interpretation.

Commercial paper. This is a general term connoting the different legal documents used in local, national, and world trade. It includes such items as checks, promissory notes, bank drafts, certificates of deposit, and other negotiable instruments. There are two types of commercial paper, non-negotiable and negotiable. In a non-negotiable paper, the debtor states that he owes a sum of money to a specific individual. He will pay the money only to that individual. In a negotiable paper, the debtor promises to pay any person to whom the paper is endorsed or transferred.

Thus, a commercial paper is negotiable if it can be transferred by endorsement or delivery. A document which states that the debtor will "pay to the Order of John Jones" can be transferred by a proper endorsement by John Jones. All checks fit into this category. Commercial paper in which the debtor promises to pay the "bearer" can be transferred by mere delivery. The debtor must pay the person who has the paper in his possession. Many corporate bonds also fall into this category.

Elements of commercial paper

In order to be negotiable, a written document must contain four elements:

1. It must be signed by the maker or drawer. The signature can be handwritten, typed, printed, or stamped. It can even be initials, a mark, or a trade name.

2. It must contain an unconditional promise to pay a definite amount of money. The following promise would be sufficient: "I promise to pay $1,000. . . ." It would not be negotiable if it read: "I promise to pay $1,000 if the profits are good this year. . . ." This is too indefinite since it is conditioned on the existence of profits. The promise must be unconditional and certain.

3. It must be payable on demand or at a definite time. Sometimes a note will say "Payable on Demand." This is sufficient. It is also sufficient if it states ". . . payable on the date of the election of a Republican president."

4. It must be payable to order or to bearer. To satisfy this requirement the note must say "Pay to the order of ______" or "Pay to Bearer." If it states pay to the order of a named individual, that person must endorse the note to transfer it. If it is "bearer" paper, it can be negotiated by mere delivery. No endorsement is needed. When "Pay to the order of *Cash*" is written on a check it becomes bearer paper and does not require an endorsement to transfer it.

Documents containing these four elements are negotiable commercial paper. Negotiable documents are the only commercial papers traded on the stock exchange, over the counter, or among the banks and finance companies. It is advisible for the layman to know the elements of this type of paper and the results which may flow from its use.

Types of commercial paper

Many different commercial papers are used in the financial and trade markets. Everyone has contact with some form of commercial paper, such as checks. Other commercial papers are less common and are often called negotiable instruments. These documents include the following:

Bonds. A bond is a formal certificate of indebtedness in which the debtor promises to pay a certain amount of money on a definite date. For example, a corporate bond may be issued in a certificate for the amount of $1,000, due and payable on July 1, 1990. Different bonds include governmental, such as municipal, "E," "H," and savings; and private, corporate, industrial, and commercial bonds.

Certificate of deposit. This is a commercial banking method by which the depositor agrees to place a definite amount of money in the bank for a specific period of time. It is similar to a bond in that it contains the bank's promise to pay the depositor the amount of money plus interest on a specified date. A certificate of deposit has the advantage of earning a higher rate of interest than other saving plans. However, the depositor is unable to withdraw his money during the specified period of deposit.

Promissory note. One of the most common negotiable instruments is the promissory note. This is a written document in which one person promises to pay to the order or to the bearer a specified sum of money on demand or at a definite date. All home and auto loans financed by commercial banks are premised on promissory notes.

Bill of exchange. This document, which is also called a "draft," is "an unconditional order in writing addressed by one person to another, signed by the person giving it, requiring the person to whom it is addressed to pay on demand or at a fixed . . . time a sum certain in money to order or to bearer."

Checks. An ordinary check is the most common example of a bill of exchange. As the Uniform Commercial Code defines it, a check "is a draft drawn on a bank and payable on demand." In legal terms it is a written order addressed to the bank and signed by the depositor. It orders the bank to pay a certain amount of money to a specific individual. Unlike a promissory note in which there are only two parties, a check or draft is generally a three-party instrument. In other words the writer orders the bank to pay the bearer a certain amount of money.

In addition to regular checks, banks also offer *certified checks*. A bank will guarantee the validity of a signature on a certified check. Furthermore, as soon as the check is certified, the bank deducts an equal amount from the depositor's account. At this point the bank has assumed total responsibility and is directly liable for the check. There is no special form for a certified check. The bank merely stamps "CERTIFIED" on the face of the depositor's normal check blank.

On the other hand, a *cashier's check* is drawn directly on the bank's account. An individual can walk into a bank and purchase cashier's checks with cash, or with a check on his own account. A cashier's check is used when the customer desires a record and a mode of payment which the creditor will accept.

Transfer of checks

When a person receives a check, he generally puts it in the bank. From a legal standpoint, the check is addressed: "Pay to the Order of *John Jones*." In order for Jones to deposit it, he must endorse the check on the back. There are several rules regarding different methods of endorsement and the results they effect. These include:

Blank. To effect a blank endorsement, the person to whom

it is addressed signs his name on the back of the check. Once it is endorsed in this manner, it becomes bearer paper. Anyone holding the check can collect on it. No further endorsements are required. Thus, if the face of the check said "Pay to the Order of *John Jones*," the check would become bearer paper as soon as John Jones endorsed it.

Special. In a special endorsement, the first payee names a specific person to whom the bank must pay the amount of the check. If, in our above example, John Jones had endorsed the check by writing "Pay Carl Smith" on the back he would have made a special endorsement. In order to further transfer the check, Carl Smith would have to sign his own name under the first endorsement.

This form of endorsement provides the payee with some protection by requiring the bank to pay a specific individual. However, the check can become bearer paper if that person endorses it.

Restrictive. If John Jones endorses his check "For Deposit only, John Jones," he has written a restrictive endorsement. Once endorsed in this manner, the check can only be transferred by depositing it in the name of the person who endorsed the check. The safety implications of this legal rule are immediately apparent. If a check has a restrictive endorsement, it virtually cannot be passed on. Hence, when checks of this type are stolen, they are of no use to the criminal. If the person wishes to be doubly safe, he can endorse the check "For Deposit Only in ABC Bank, John Jones." This is a special restrictive endorsement because it names the specific bank and it limits the manner (deposit) by which the check can be transferred.

Qualified. By a qualified endorsement, the signer limits his liability on the instrument. An endorsement signed "Without Recourse, John Jones" is a qualified instrument. For example, suppose Baker gives Jones a check. Jones endorses the check using the statement, "without recourse," and gives it to Smith. When Smith attempts to collect, the check is returned with a note that Baker's account has "Insufficient Funds." Normally, Smith would be allowed to collect from Jones. However, the qualified endorsement means that Smith has no recourse to Jones. Jones has limited his liability and stated that he will not pay if Baker does not pay. The disadvantage in this form of endorsement is clear. In most cases, it is best to avoid accepting any negotiable instrument with a qualified endorsement.

Holder in due course

Earlier in the chapter, the elements of a valid commercial paper or negotiable instrument were discussed. If these factors are present, the document is a negotiable instrument. This is an important determination in that a holder of such paper has special rights in the legal and commercial world. One who has lawful possession of a negotiable instrument is known as a "holder in due course." This person must have given something valuable for the document in good faith and without any knowledge of legal deficiencies in the note. The holder in due course has important legal protection. When he takes possession of the negotiable instrument he is not bound by any of the defenses granted by law to the original promisor. To illustrate:

> "A" buys a color television from "B" and gives B a negotiable promissory note for $500 in payment for it. "B" sells the note to "C Finance Company" for $490. As such, "C Finance Company" has become a holder in due course. The television is delivered, but never works. Consequently "A" tells "B" he will not pay. If "B" still held the note, the defense of nonperformance would be valid. But "C" now has the note. The fact that the television does not work is of no concern to "C"; he is a holder in due course. Therefore, if "C" brings "A" into court to enforce payment, he is free from any charges by "A" that the original contract was not performed.

The law clearly works to the advantage of the commercial companies and the holders in due course. It is a harsh rule when applied to a person who is left with a television that does not work and a $500 promissory note which he still must pay. Thus, legal experts strongly advise the layman to remember this principle when signing a credit contract. A careful reading of any contract on credit agreement will forewarn the customer that the paper may be transferred to another person. In many cases he can ask for a restrictive clause to prohibit any commercial transfer. If the problem is more complicated or if the individual has further questions, he should seek professional advice.

Safe deposit box

A final area in which the layman may become involved in a bank's business is through the rental of a safe deposit box. Most banks maintain a special vault which houses individual safe deposit boxes. These boxes can be rented by the bank's customers for a small annual amount.

Safe deposit box contracts may be individual or joint. If it is an individual contract, only that individual can gain access to the rented box. Under a *joint contract,* either of the two renters may open the box. It is not necessary that both persons be present.

The most important legal questions arise when the renter dies. In most instances, if the contract is individual, the box must be inventoried for state tax and inheritance laws before the executor can distribute the proceeds of the box.

If the safe deposit box is under a joint contract, the legal situation is more complex. The laws of the various states differ as to the effect of the death of one of the renters. Some states permit the surviving joint renter unlimited access to the safe deposit box. Other states have laws which seal the box pending an inventory by state tax agents. Still other states permit limited access in order to look for a will, burial instructions, and insurance policies.

It is important to remember that most safe deposit contracts do not automatically include insurance for the contents. This must be handled independently. Usually a rider can be attached to a homeowner's policy with little cost in time or expense. The individual's regular insurance agent

can advise him on the best method.

Finally, what documents should be kept in a safe deposit box? Experts recommend that bonds, stock certificates, important records relating to the individual's property, mortgages, titles, and deeds be put in a safe deposit box. These items can be replaced, but only after considerable aggravation and sometimes substantial cost.

It is also useful to include important personal papers in the contents of the box. Such papers include birth certificates, marriage certificates, and death certificates. Military records, important church or synagogue records, valid passports, and any citizenship papers. Important contracts and automobile titles are other significant papers that should be included.

Important insurance policies, such as life and fire, are best kept in a locked safe deposit box. Also, in the event of theft, fire or any other disaster, the individual is better protected if he has an inventory of his household possessions in his locked box. Without a list, faulty memories may cause the homeowner to suffer a larger loss than that against which he had been protected.

Most experts doubt the advisability of keeping a will in a safe deposit box. Although most states permit removal for estate administration purposes, these processes sometimes cause undesired delay. According to legal experts, the better procedure is to keep a *copy* of the will in the safe deposit box. The original should be retained by the individual or given to an attorney or the future executor. This will insure that estate administration begins at the earliest possible moment.

Knowledge of the legal rules and principles applicable to banking could prove useful in saving money and avoiding problems in the management of personal business and commercial affairs.

Chapter Eight

Tax Troubles

The number of Americans who file tax returns on or before April 15 of each year now runs to about 80 million. About 4 percent, or 3 million persons, have their tax returns audited or examined by the Internal Revenue Service.

All income tax returns are checked for mathematical accuracy. The taxpayer is notified of any error which results in a tax rebate or in a bill for an additional tax. In general, the Internal Revenue Service closely examines or audits those returns which indicate:

- An adjusted gross income over $25,000
- A large income of deduction items
- Any unusual transactions
- Any unexplained items on the return
- Difference between income reported and the information contained in W-2 Forms and 1099 Informational Forms

In addition, the Internal Revenue Service closely scrutinizes returns which have been flagged because of a letter from an informer indicating that a taxpayer may be attempting to circumvent the law.

If you are notified of an audit by the Internal Revenue Service, you will be advised to bring all your tax records to the tax department or to a nearby Internal Revenue Service agent. These records normally include bills, canceled checks, and other written records and inventories that are relevant to your tax return. If your return was prepared by an attorney or certified public accountant, you should notify him before meeting with the Internal Revenue Service. You may, of course, ask your own accountant or attorney to accompany you.

If the Internal Revenue Service agent determines that your records are in error, you have thirty days in which to appeal his decision to the District Audit Division Conference. If the District Conference produces an adverse decision, the taxpayer can further appeal his case to the Appellate Division of the Office of the Regional Commissioner. If the Internal Revenue appellant officer hearing your appeal determines that there has been a "deficiency" in the amount of taxes which you have paid, he issues what is commonly called the "ninety-day letter." Before the end of ninety days, the taxpayer has the choice of paying the tax or petitioning the Tax Court of the United States to hear his appeal.

If the tax problem is of any consequence or complexity, the taxpayer will normally seek the services of a tax attorney or a certified public accountant admitted to practice before the Tax Court of the United States.

The tax court has also established a new simplified procedure for small taxpayers to handle their own cases before the tax court. On a simple form, the taxpayer can petition the tax court, giving the necessary information as to the date of the receipt of the deficiency letter, the address of the nearest regional office of the Internal Revenue Service, and the amount of the deficiency or disputed tax. This small tax case procedure has a maximum limit of $1,000 for the amount of tax in dispute. The reasons why the taxpayer believes the additional tax is not due must also be included. The petition must be signed by the husband and the wife if both are joining in the filing of the petition. A filing fee of ten dollars must accompany the original. It must be filed by the nineteenth day or it cannot be considered.

This procedure permits the small taxpayer to bring his own case before the court. Previously, the argument was often made that only the rich could afford tax disputes. This new procedure permits the average taxpayer to fight the authorities.

There is a "statute of limitations" which establishes a period within which the Internal Revenue Service can act to propose changes on your return or, in the case of a fraudulent return, start prosecution of criminal charges. In the case of simple matters not involving fraud or gross understatement of income, the government must act within three years of the due date of the filing of the return or they are barred from acting. If the return is filed after April 15th, the three-year period starts from the time the return is filed.

In a case of fraud or international tax evasion the government's period within which to act is *six* years from the time the return was filed or the due date of the return, whichever is later.

The regulations provide many civil and criminal penalties for violations of the income tax laws. For a willful failure to file a return, the law imposes a penalty of 5 percent on the unpaid tax *per month* for each month's delay, up to a maximum of 25 percent. If it is a simple failure to pay the tax on time, the penalty is 6 percent of the unpaid tax per year, plus interest. If the tax payment is made with a bad check, the Internal Revenue Service imposes an additional penalty of 1 percent of the check. In addition to the civil penalties, the law also has criminal penalties. For a willful failure to file a return to pay a tax, the law may impose the criminal penalty of a $10,000 fine or imprisonment of up to one year, or both. For a willful attempt to evade taxes, the punishment is a fine of up to $10,000 or imprisonment up to five years, or both. For signing a tax return which you know to be false, you may be subjected to a fine of $5,000 or up to three years' imprisonment, or both. As you can readily see, the penalties, both civil and criminal, are stringent. Thus it is important to prepare your tax returns so as not to violate these rules.

If you are ever contacted by a "Special Agent" of the Internal Revenue Service he will usually advise you that he is examining your return to determine whether or not you have committed a crime in your income tax return. In such a case you should *always* seek the the immediate assistance of an attorney experienced in this field. Do not become involved in any discussions with the agent. Tell him to "see your lawyer."

Federal and state governments are updating their methods of keeping track of both evasive and delinquent taxpayers. Many states have adopted a broad state-federal agreement which provides for a sharing of information on nearly all forms of taxation. This should improve both tax collection and enforcement of tax laws. These federal-state agreements, subscribed to by every state except Alabama, Connecticut, Louisiana, Nevada, Rhode Island, and Texas, provide for sharing of enforcement, personnel training, audit procedures, and mutual assistance. Parties to the agreement will be able to inspect taxpayer lists, computer tapes, and other information concerning delinquent taxpayers. The use of this type of agreement should further reduce the incidence of failure to pay taxes and the evasion of full payment. In view of these new arrangements, backed by modern methods of computer, microfilm, and machine-readers, few can expect to cheat the system and get away with it.

The complexity of the tax rules and regulations defies simplification. Effective resolution of a specific problem depends on the facts and circumstances surrounding it. In many instances, this may require professional advisors, such as a personal lawyer or a certified public accountant. However, many tax problems may be solved through diligent homework by the taxpayer and the information secured from a representative of the Internal Revenue Service.

Chapter Nine

Law and the Family

The law of domestic relations defines the rights and responsibilities of the individual with respect to marriage and the family. Each state governs family situations that fall within its jurisdiction. In general, state statutes prescribe the legal qualifications for marriage, the grounds for divorce or separation, and the extent to which family members are required to support each other. Although these provisions differ in specific instances among the various states, a description of the laws applicable in a majority of states can provide the reader with a general knowledge of this subject.

Marriage

Marriage is a legal as well as a social relationship. Socially, it is an essential part of our society's structure in that it forms the basic family unit. Legally, it is a civil contract entered into by two consenting and capable parties. Unlike other contracts, however, it cannot be terminated at will by the two persons involved. Unless the bond is dissolved by the state, it is binding until the death of one of the parties. Furthermore, the law states that the marriage relationship can exist between only one man and one woman at a time.

The validity of a marriage is determined by the laws of the state in which it takes place. Since the requirements for marriage differ among the various states, a marriage that is legal where it took place is recognized anywhere in the United States.

In order for a marriage to be valid, the individuals must be legally, mentally, and physically capable of entering into the contract. In addition, each party must consent to the marriage.

Legally, two persons may be incapable of marrying if one or both are under age, if they are closely related, or if one of the persons is bound by a previous, undissolved marriage. A marriage that takes place under any of these circumstances is either void or voidable.

For example, a marriage between persons who are under age may not be legal. Ordinarily, it is recognized unless one of the parties elects to have it set aside. In general, females must be sixteen and males, eighteen before they can consent to marriage. Furthermore, in some states, females must be eighteen and males, twenty-one before they can marry without the consent of a parent or guardian.

A marriage between persons who are more closely related than cousins is void. For example, a marriage between an uncle and niece would automatically be set aside. A marriage that takes place while one of the parties is still legally married also is void.

Mental incompetency also can render a marriage invalid. Mental incapacities include insanity, imbecility, intoxication, and similar conditions that deprive a person of his reason. A marriage contracted while one of the parties is mentally incapacitated is voidable. However, that person can ratify the marriage if he or she, subsequently, regains competency.

It is essential that both parties consent to the marriage. If one of the parties agrees to the marriage under duress, the court may declare it null and void. Furthermore, if one of the parties is not aware that the ceremony is a marriage rite, that person has not consented to marriage. In general, the court will allow the uninformed or mistaken party to have the marriage declared void.

Nearly a third of the states recognize common-law marriage. This is an agreement whereby a man and a woman consent to live together as husband and wife without an official ceremony. No certificate or license is required. No formal contract is created. The continuing existence of the marriage is contingent upon the parties' intent to remain together.

Responsibilities of husband and wife

The legal relationship of marriage creates certain obligations for both parties. Theoretically, the husband is the head of the household. It is his duty to support and provide for his wife and family. In return, according to common-law theory, the wife is supposed to render service to her husband.

The husband is obliged to support his wife although she may have property and earnings of her own. However, this duty exists only while they live together as man and wife. If they separate due to the wife's actions, the husband is not required to continue support. On the other hand, if the husband is responsible or if both desire a separation, the husband is obliged to provide for the wife.

Among his responsibilities is the husband's duty to provide his wife and family with the necessities of life. This legal rule has evolved into the "doctrine of necessaries."

Thus, without her husband's knowledge or consent, a wife can purchase *necessary* food and clothing for herself and her children and charge their cost to her husband. Although he may not have authorized the purchases, the husband must pay the bills.

In addition to the common necessities of food, clothing, and shelter, many courts require the husband to maintain his family in accordance with his economic position. In this case, the law also imposes an obligation upon the husband to provide medical and dental care, household furniture and supplies, and certain legal services.

The husband is not automatically required to pay for luxury items. In order to impose liability on him for nonnecessaries such as fur coats, television sets, or stereos, the wife must prove that her husband gave her "apparent" authorization. For example, Mr. Smith informs a merchant he will pay for his wife's purchases. Thus the merchant extends credit to her. After an argument, Smith tells his wife that she can no longer purchase anything on credit but neglects to notify the merchant of this change of authority. Therefore, when Mrs. Smith comes in to charge some items, the merchant is perfectly reasonable in granting her credit. To his knowledge, she still has authority to buy on credit. This is true even though Smith has revoked her actual authority.

Actual authority is clearer and more common. For example, Smith signs a charge account statement in which he agrees to pay for any items charged to that account. If Mrs. Smith has use of the charge account, her husband will be fully liable for her purchases.

Traditionally, the wife is expected to perform household and other tasks for her husband. These services are to be rendered "free." For example, a husband can sue to recover damages for the "loss of his wife's services" if she is injured by the negligent action of another.

Rights of husband and wife

Under common law, husband and wife formerly were considered one person. Under this theory, the wife had no property rights. Today, all state legislatures have modified, if not eliminated, this legal unity of husband and wife. The wife now has rights to property, the right to make contracts, and the right to sue.

Since the husband is considered the head of the household, he has the legal right to choose the place of residence for his family. The wife is obligated to follow him to the new address. Moreover, in the absence of a special direction to the contrary, the husband owns the household goods. Wedding gifts belong to both husband and wife.

However, if a specific present is particularly suited to use by one of the parties, that person may claim it.

When a husband and wife purchase real estate, they are commonly known as "tenants by the entirety." According to this common-law rule they both own the whole property. Neither can transfer his half to another party. Thus, if one of the owners wishes to sell his interest in the property he (or she) must obtain the consent of his (or her) spouse.

Property owned in this manner is not good security for a creditor with a claim against one of the tenants since upon the death of one spouse the entire property passes to the surviving owner. If the creditor wins his claim in court, and files the judgment as a lien against the debtor's interest in the property, the lien attaches to the survivorship interest of the partner who is his debtor. For example, if the creditor's claim is against the wife, his judgment attaches to her interest in the property, but he can levy against the property only if the wife survives her husband. If she dies first, his security is worthless.

Marriage settlements relate solely to property. These agreements can be made either before or after the marriage takes place. In general, a settlement is made by persons with property rights that would be affected by marriage. However, it cannot affect the obligations of matrimony. For instance, a husband cannot use a settlement to limit his wife's annual allowance for clothing and incidentals. On the other hand, he can provide by settlement that his wife will receive a stated share of his wealth or interest in his property.

In general, any property acquired by the wife during marriage is her own. For instance, if she wins a lawsuit for a certain amount of money, that sum is hers to keep or use as she likes. Several states, however, have adopted the community property system. Under these laws, all property obtained through the efforts of either person or through the work of both belongs to both husband and wife. Separate property can be acquired during marriage only by gift or inheritance. Property owned by one spouse before marriage remains the property of that individual. Also, income derived from separate property during marriage is also separate property.

Among other rights, the wife is entitled to sue a third party for damages if she has suffered an injury to her person, property, or reputation through an act of that person. In some cases, the husband also may sue for damages because of the loss of his wife's services.

In most states, the wife retains the right to conduct business activities on her own. In a few states, however, she must petition the court in order to obtain this right without restriction.

Support of children

Generally speaking, parents are obligated by law to support and protect their children. In addition, they are required to see that their offspring are educated in accordance with state laws. If parents are totally lacking in funds, the obligation to educate will end when the child completes the minimum state educational requirements. However, if the family is financially secure, a particular state may require a parent to send his children to college and to pay all the necessary expenses. An individual attorney in the reader's state will be able to inform him of the legal requirements of that state, as well as the extent to which the courts have enforced these laws.

According to traditional common law in the United States, the father is primarily responsible for the support of his children. If he is unable or refuses to support them, the mother is secondarily responsible for their support. Normally, the duty to support a child continues until the child reaches majority. In most states this is the age of twenty-one. Consequently, in most states, a child is legally permitted to seek a court order requiring his father to make specific support payments according to an established timetable.

At first glance, this principle may appear to condone parent-support payments to children who lead undisciplined lives away from home. This may not be the case, however. Some state courts will not require parents to support children who live away from the family residence if it is shown that the father is willing and able to support his offspring in his own home. Thus, suppose Jimmy Smith, age seventeen, wishes to lead a "free" existence away from home. He asks that the court order his father to send him periodic payments for his support. If it is demonstrated that Jimmy's father is able and willing to support his son at home, the court may not require Smith to make any support payments that would underwrite Jimmy's existence in another environment.

Problems involving divorce proceedings account for most of the legal cases relating to child support. In many divorce proceedings, a portion of the divorce decree includes a child-support order requiring the father to provide for his child.

The first element in formulating child-support orders is the determination of the amount to be awarded. Generally, the judge bases this decision on evidence revealing the respective parents' financial resources. The goal of the court is to provide the child with sufficient money so that he may be raised in an atmosphere which reflects his parents' standard of living before the divorce. Thus, the general rule is the wealthier the father, the larger the child-support payments.

Child-support payments do not last indefinitely. Usually the court order states that the payments will continue until the child reaches his majority. However, under certain circumstances, the court will require a father to support his adult offspring. Thus, if a child is physically disabled, mentally retarded, or otherwise unable to care for himself, local law may require the parent to continue support payments throughout the life of the child. The court's paramount concern at all times is the welfare of the child.

Child-support payments are always subject to modification. A court will terminate support payments before the child reaches twenty-one (majority) if the child has become "emancipated" or self-supporting. Examples of emancipation include marriage; military service; and full-time, self-supporting jobs. A child's emancipation terminates the father's duties in all situations, not merely those involving divorce.

For many of America's youth, a college education is a "necessity" for adult financial success and personal achievement. Consequently, when a court issues child-support orders it often must consider whether the father should be required to pay for his children's college expenses. The traditional view, which is still prevalent in a majority of states, requires the father to furnish only the minimum amount of compulsory education.

However, some states are taking a different approach. These courts officially recognize the need to adequately prepare the child to meet the complexities of modern society. Under this view, if the father is financially able and the child shows a certain aptitude, the court will order the father to pay for the child's college education. This new approach is gaining increased acceptance. Furthermore, some courts require support payments beyond the date of the child's majority, thereby allowing him to finish his education.

Termination of marriage

Because the marriage contract is protected by the state and because the state laws governing this relationship are diverse, marriage is often difficult to terminate. The only way it can be dissolved before the death of one of the parties is by a judicial act. Basically, there are three legal methods by which the contract may be dissolved or suspended:

• *Divorce* is the basic judicial act which dissolves a marriage. An *absolute divorce* completely breaks the bonds of matrimony. A *limited divorce,* also known as a *judicial* or *legal separation,* suspends the marriage relation. The husband must provide for the separate maintenance of his wife.

• *Voluntary separation* occurs when husband and wife agree to live apart. It often results in a separation agreement. This document includes provisions for the support of the wife and for the custody and support of any children.

• *Annulment* is the result of a court decree. It declares the marriage invalid from its inception. An annulment differs from a divorce in that it usually must be based on a reason or cause that existed at the time of marriage.

Divorce

A decree of divorce legally obtained in one state is enforceable in all other states. However, the state granting the divorce must have jurisdiction over the action and the parties involved. Every state has judicial control over citizens residing within its borders. Hence, a divorce or separation rendered by a particular state in an action involving its residents is binding anywhere in the United States. Anyone seeking to obtain a divorce in a state other than his own should learn the jurisdictional requirements of that state before seeking a decision there. For example, almost all states have minimum residency requirements. Although most states have laws discouraging "quick" divorces, several states allow easy divorces. For example, Idaho and Nevada both have residency requirements of six weeks.

If the person seeking the divorce fulfills the requirements of that state, the decree normally will be binding. However, it is important to remember that every state has the right to determine whether another state had the authority to grant a particular divorce before it is obligated to accept that decree.

Grounds for divorce

Although states have different policies, there are certain major causes or reasons for divorce. They include the following:

• *Adultery* is a universal ground for divorce in the United States. However, some states stipulate that a single act of adultery is not a sufficient basis for divorce.

• *Conviction of certain crimes* is grounds for divorce in about forty states. Also, imprisonment in a prison or federal penitentiary for a certain number of years can constitute grounds for a divorce.

• *Extreme cruelty* of one kind or another is a basis for divorce in most states. Cruelty includes acts of violence; constantly offensive language that causes mental anguish; conduct imposing hardship, conduct that injures health; communication of disease; and habitual intemperance.

• *Desertion* is the separation of one spouse from another without justification, without consent, and with no intentions of returning.

• *Insanity or idiocy* is a ground for divorce in many states.

• *Impotence* is a basis for divorce in many states. If the condition exists at the time of marriage it constitutes a cause of action for annulment.

• *Nonsupport* of wife consists of a husband's refusal to provide his wife with suitable support. Generally, it must continue for at least a year to be considered grounds for divorce.

• *Violent and ungovernable temper* is a basis for divorce in some states. However, the outbursts must be so frequent and violent as to affect the health, safety, or comfort of the complaining spouse.

• Other grounds for divorce include *fraud* or concealment of some fact essential to the validity of the marriage; marriage under duress or a forced marriage; incompatibility; and pregnancy at the time of marriage if the father is not the prospective husband.

Defenses to divorce actions

A divorce is not always granted when a seemingly appropriate cause is presented. Often there are extenuating circumstances that justify or excuse the act of the offending spouse. These constitute defenses to the action. They include the following:

• *Condonation* occurs when one spouse forgives a matrimonial offense of the other. For example, if a husband learns that his wife has committed adultery but continues to live with her, he has condoned the offense. He no longer has grounds for a divorce action.

• *Provocation and justification.* When one spouse seeks a divorce on the basis of cruelty, nonsupport, or desertion, the defendant may be able to prove misconduct on the part of the complaining party and thereby defeat the divorce action.

• *Collusion.* If a husband and wife agree that one will commit a matrimonial offense so that the other can obtain a divorce, they have committed a fraud against the court. If one spouse changes his mind and reveals this collusion, the court may deny the divorce.

Separation

A husband and wife may separate with or without a judicial decree. Unlike a divorce, marital separation is not necessarily permanent. The chance of reconciliation remains. *Voluntary separation* occurs when a husband and wife agree to live apart. In many cases, this form of separation may give rise to a formal settlement agreement.

• *Settlement agreements.* If a husband and wife are unable to reconcile their differences after living apart for a while, they may decide to draw up a separation agreement. This document states that the parties intend to live separate and apart, provides settlement of property rights, declares that the parties are not to interfere with each other, and provides for the custody, control, and support of any children.

• *Judicial separation.* In order to sustain an action for judicial separation, the complaining spouse must show grounds as prescribed by the laws of that state. In some states, a legal separation is granted for any of the reasons for which a divorce is decreed. In most states, desertion and cruelty constitute causes of action for separation. However, each state prescribes specific and often different grounds for this form of "limited" divorce.

Custody of children

The court has the power to award custody and control of children temporarily pending the outcome of a divorce action and at the conclusion of divorce, separation, and annulment proceedings. The court's decision is based on the welfare of the child. The desires of the parents and of the children must yield to the judgment of the court.

Under common law, the father usually was granted custody of the children. Modern court policy, however, is to give the mother custody of the children unless she is unfit or incapable of caring for them. However, many courts follow a rule of awarding custody to the innocent party in a divorce action.

Alimony

The husband is required to give his wife alimony or separate maintenance payments after the issuance of the following documents:

1) A court decree of divorce or separate maintenance or a written instrument incidental to such a decree.

2) A written separation agreement; or

3) A court decree for support.

The court awards the wife temporary alimony while the case is pending. After the conclusion of the case, the court requires the husband to pay a permanent allowance for his wife's support and maintenance. In general, a court order providing for alimony specifies that payments will cease if the wife remarries.

Some states limit alimony to a certain percentage of the husband's income. In other states, the policy is to award the wife a specific amount that can be paid in one lump sum or in installments. States operating under the community property system can divide the property of the married couple and attach the property of the husband to insure payment of alimony. In general, courts consider all the circumstances of both husband and wife before determining the amount of alimony. Basically, these include the age and health of both parties, their earning capacities, the personal wealth of both parties, and their conduct in relation to the divorce action.

In most states, the court will hold the husband in contempt of court if he fails to pay the alimony. The husband may be imprisoned for civil contempt until he agrees to pay.

The breach of a separation agreement by the husband is the same as a breach of contract. Thus, the legal steps used to force the fulfillment of a contract are applicable to this situation also.

Other family support obligations

The traditional common law of family support obligations concerned only husband, wife, and children. According to this law, marriage formed a family unit. Consequently, the husband was no longer legally obligated to support his parents, and his parents no longer had a legal duty to support him. However, this concept is changing.

Most states have enacted laws requiring residents to support their parents. These statutes are applied when a parent or parents are unable to take care of themselves financially or physically. If a parent has been placed in a state welfare institution, the state can institute court proceedings to get a parental support order. This order directs children to pay the cost of maintaining their parents in the institution.

Although the majority of Americans voluntarily contribute to their parents' support if the situation so requires, the laws requiring support are on the books. It is important to be aware of them in the event that an individual is faced with such a problem.

Whenever a family or marital problem is taken to court, tremendous pressure and strain are placed on the individuals involved. Sometimes personal relations are completely severed. When a situation of this nature arises, the concerned parties often find it difficult to act reasonably. This chapter will not solve any specific problems, but it may help the individual to recognize a legal problem if one arises. He can then seek professional advice to learn the possible legal and financial ramifications of the law's application in his particular case.

Chapter Ten

Law and Your Property

Private ownership of property is an integral part of our American system. Today, over 60 percent of all American families own their homes. In a typical year, 4.5 million Americans buy houses. This is an average of one sale every ten seconds. For these reasons, a basic understanding of real property law is becoming increasingly useful.

The concept of real property includes land and anything erected on it, growing on it, or permanently connected with it so as to be immovable. Thus, buildings, trees, and any permanent fixtures such as swimming pools are part of this property. Real property differs from personal property which consists of movable items such as appliances, carpets, drapes, and furniture.

The law of real property covers all rights and liabilities incident to the purchase, sale, possession, and ownership of real estate.

Ownership of real estate

What does it mean to *own* a piece of land? In common usage, ownership is equated with an absolute title to the land. In other words, the owner has sole title to the property. Strictly speaking, however, an individual seldom has a perfect title. Usually ownership connotes having a *marketable title.* This means that the title has no serious legal defect. It may have minor legal flaws, but these are not serious enough to impede its marketability.

One might ask how there can be flaws in a title and why one cannot obtain a perfect title. A partial answer can be drawn from this example:

> "A," owner of Whiteacre, abandons the property. Consequently, "B" adversely possesses the property for twenty-five years. At this point, as between "A" and "B," "B" has the better title, although neither has a perfect title. To complicate the situation further, suppose "A" makes a provision in his will that "C" shall have rights to the property for twenty years and that thereafter "D" and his descendants shall have it. Before "B" dies, he mortgages the property to a bank and defaults. "B" then dies and the estate wishes to sell the property.

It is clear that the purchaser of the property can never have a perfect title. However, the purchaser can have a marketable title by securing releases from every individual with an interest in the property. In the above example, a marketable title would require formal written releases from "A's" descendants, from the bank, from "C," and from "D" and his descendants.

How does the purchaser know if he has a marketable title? This is solved by the *title search* which requires an examination of the official county land records to determine the chain of title. This examination should disclose all transactions involving the land, as well as all tax assessments which may have been levied but not paid. Once the search is completed, the necessary releases can be executed and a marketable title can be constructed.

Years ago, the individual's lawyer conducted the title search by examining all the official records relating to the property. In a few isolated areas, this function is still performed by lawyers. Generally, however, independent abstract companies now conduct the title search. Because they maintain a duplicate set of property records, these companies are able to give the customer an abstract, or digest, of the essential recorded facts concerning that specific property.

The lawyer uses the abstract to form a legal opinion on the marketability of the title. Using this information he can determine whether any releases need be sought and whether any formal legal proceedings are required to obtain a marketable title. When the lawyer has finished this task, the purchaser will have a marketable title.

If he wishes to further safeguard his interests, the individual can acquire title insurance for his property. It is available in most states. For a relatively small amount, a title insurance company will guarantee the title against any defects. The company will also defend the new owner against any unfounded claims on the title. Title insurance is widely accepted in this country and significantly increases the security of the property owner.

Claims against property

The concept of laying claim against real property to insure the payment of a debt is an important aspect of real estate law. Mortgages, tax liens, mechanics' liens, judgment liens, and attachment liens are all legal tools that can be used to force payment of a debt. In each case the real property subject to the lien serves as security for the money owed by the property owner.

Mortgage

Few families can afford to pay cash for their homes. The majority borrow a large sum of money to finance their purchase. A *mortgage* is legally defined as a formal pledge of property to secure the repayment of this loan. The *mortgagor* is the owner of the property that is pledged as security. The *mortgagee* is the lender of the money.

For example, Central Bank loans Jones $20,000 so that he can purchase his new three-bedroom home. In return, Jones executes a promissory note to Central Bank for $20,000 plus the stated amount of interest. In addition, he pledges, or mortgages, the property as security for his promise to repay the loan. If Jones is unable to maintain the payments, he defaults on the mortgage. A default gives Central Bank the right to *foreclose*. In other words, the bank can institute a legal proceeding to sell the property and regain its money.

The concept of the mortgage dates back to ancient common law. Early Anglo-American common law decreed that a mortgage conveyed an absolute interest in the property to the lender or mortgagee. In other words, the mortgagee had actual title to the property during the period of the outstanding loan. Of course, the mortgagee could not transfer possession of the property to a third person unless the mortgagor defaulted in his payments. Moreover, when the mortgagor completed his payments, he regained the actual title. This is known as the "title" theory of mortgage and some states still adhere to it.

The "title" theory is somewhat analogous to the automobile loan situation. When an individual buys an automobile on credit, he signs a sales contract agreeing to give the finance company or bank legal title to the car until the loan is repaid. Then the title is transferred to the purchaser. The car is the security for the loan. In the home mortgage situation, the house is security for the loan.

The counterpart to the title theory is the "lien" theory. Under this doctrine, the title to the property remains with the purchaser and the lender has only a "lien" on the property. However, if the buyer defaults in this situation, the lender still maintains his right to enforce his lien on the property by foreclosing.

A typical mortgage consists of two separate legal documents. The debt itself is evidenced by a signed written note in which the purchaser promises to repay the principal amount of the loan and the stated interest on that amount. In a separate document, the purchaser pledges his property as security for his promise to make the monthly mortgage payments. In effect he says, "If I do not keep my promise to pay $195 per month for the next twenty years, I authorize you to sell my property and collect whatever money is needed to pay off the loan."

Many people are aware of the three categories of home loans: Veterans Administration (VA) loans, Federal Housing Administration (FHA) loans, and conventional loans. The VA and FHA loans are guaranteed by the federal government, while the conventional loan is solely between the lender and the borrower. Most people think of these terms when asked about the different types of mortgages. Legally, however, there are other differences between mortgages.

The legal types of mortgages include the normal loan by a lending institution, the purchase money mortgage or vendor's lien, and the construction mortgage. The first type has already been discussed. In the purchase money mortgage, the purchaser borrows money in order to buy the property that serves as security for the loan. He agrees to pay the seller a stated amount over a period of years. If the purchaser defaults, the vendor or seller has the right to recover the unpaid purchase money.

In the home-improvement or construction mortgage, the lender often makes pro rata advances of the loan as the construction or renovation is completed. Thus, there may be a schedule according to which the lender releases $2,000 for the basic frame structure, $2,000 after the completion of the roof, another $2,000 when the plumbing and electrical wiring is completed, and so on. However, aside from the step-by-step release of the loan, this mortgage is the same as any other. Once the entire amount of the loan has been released, the owner must maintain his monthly payments or the lender can foreclose.

Most homes are financed by a single mortgage in which a financial institution lends the purchaser a substantial portion of the purchase price. However, there are circumstances that require a second mortgage. For example, suppose, Porter sells his home to Wilson for $35,000. At the time of the sale, Porter still owes $20,000 of his mortgage loan to Central Home Loan Association. The purchaser assumes, or takes over, that loan. However, Wilson is able to pay only $5,000 in cash to Porter. He still must pay the remaining $10,000 of the purchase price. Thus, Wilson goes to National Bank and secures a second mortgage for $10,000.

There is an important legal difference between the first and second mortgage. The rights of the second lender are subordinated to those of the first. To illustrate, suppose Wilson defaults on his monthly mortgage payments to both lenders. A foreclosure proceeding is instituted and the property is sold for $25,000. The first lender, Central Home Loan Association, has the primary right to apply this money to the outstanding debt on the first mortgage. If Wilson still owes $18,000 on the first mortgage, this amount of the foreclosure sale price will be used to satisfy the first mortgage. Any remaining money will be applied to paying off the second mortgage.

In this example, suppose Wilson still owes $9,000 on his second mortgage. However, the amount left from the auc-

tion after the first mortgage has been satisfied is only $7,500. Thus, the second lender, National Bank, gets only $7,500. This example illustrates the risks to the lender inherent in a second mortgage situation. Consequently, lenders will only grant second mortgages if the debtor's credit is excellent or if the value of the property greatly exceeds the sum of the first and the proposed second mortgage.

In addition to the mortgage, there are other liens on real property: tax liens, mechanic's liens, judgment liens, and attachment liens.

Tax liens

Most states impose a tax on real property based on the assessed value of the land. If the tax is unpaid, the amount due becomes a lien on the property. The state can institute a legal action to collect the money. If necessary, the property will be sold to pay the tax. Often, however, the state will be content to wait. Given the high mobility of most

Americans, it can reasonably expect the property to be transferred within the near future. The tax lien will create a defect in the title. As a result, someone will be forced to pay the tax before the new purchaser can have a marketable title.

The U. S. government also can lay claim to real property if the individual owes federal taxes. Although it is not a common practice, the property owner should be aware of this possibility in order to fully safeguard his interests.

Mechanic's lien

Under this doctrine, the law secures payment to laborers who construct buildings or otherwise improve real estate. Most states provide for this lien by statute. The purpose of the mechanic's lien is to insure that the contractors and construction workers are paid for the work they do. The mechanic's lien differs slightly from the construction mortgage discussed earlier. In a construction mortgage, the homeowner borrows money from the bank for the express purpose of constructing a new building or improving an existing structure. In a mechanic's lien, the state imposes a lien on the property to insure that the workmen and contractors are paid their just due.

Judgment lien

To illustrate this claim, suppose White wins a judgment for $50,000 against Jones in a lawsuit arising out of an automobile accident. A judgment is a debt. Thus, Jones now becomes a debtor to White. Jones owns Property "X," valued at $20,000. To help secure payment of the debt, White files a copy of the judgment in the county in which Property "X" is located. Consequently, Property "X" is subject to a judgment lien. In most cases, the property will be untransferable until the judgment is satisfied.

Attachment lien

If there is good reason to believe that the property owner will attempt either to avoid liability or to transfer the property before the judgment is entered against him, the court will permit an *attachment lien* to be entered against the property. For example, if White has reason to believe that Jones is attempting to transfer Property "X" to "a friend," the court will permit a *writ of attachment* before the judgment is entered. This document must be filed with the appropriate official. An attachment lien protects the potential creditor's rights in case he wins the judgment. Once the judgment is entered, the attachment lien is converted to a judgment lien. If Jones fails to pay the judgment, White can institute proceedings to have the property sold and the proceeds applied to the amount of the judgment.

Foreclosure

The process of selling the property to satisfy a defaulted mortgage is called a *foreclosure*. Most states have detailed statutes setting out the specific procedure for a foreclosure proceeding. In general, the court will enter an order authorizing the sale of the land if there is proof of a default in the mortgage payments. The court will oversee the actual sale as well as the disposition of the proceeds. This insures that the proper amount is given to the creditor and that the remainder is returned to the defaulting mortgagor.

Buying and selling real property

The legal implications of buying and selling real estate are important to everyone who owns or is contemplating the purchase of a home. Buying a house is normally the largest single purchase a person will make in his lifetime. Consequently, it is important that the homeowner understand the basic principles of real estate law in order to protect his investment.

If a homeowner plans to sell his home, he must first decide whether to handle the sale himself or through a real estate broker. Ordinarily this is not a legal question; it is merely the owner's personal decision. However, the sale of real estate can have expensive legal consequences. Thus, it is unwise for the individual to negotiate the sales contract himself unless he is aware of possible legal pitfalls.

For example, if the owner tells a prospective buyer that the plumbing is constructed of copper pipe when he knows that it is not, he may jeopardize the validity of the sale. If he so desires, the purchaser can bring a legal action to set aside the contract. A homeowner desiring to sell his house by himself should seek out the advice of an attorney who can advise him on the proper drafting of the purchase contract.

Real estate agents

If the owner decides to sell his home through a real estate broker, he should study the different *listing* contracts available to him. A listing is an agreement between the owner and the real estate agent. It defines the circumstances under which the agent is entitled to a commission (usually 5 to 6 percent) on the purchase price of the property. Listings can be divided into three broad categories: open, exclusive, and multiple.

• Open listing. The owner offers the listing to any and all real estate agents. Agents often are reluctant to spend time and money promoting the sale because their chances of earning the commission are diminished by the competition of other agents.

• Exclusive listing. There are two types of exclusive listings. An "exclusive agency" lists only one real estate agent. However, the owner can sell the property himself without paying a commission to the agent. An "exclusive right to sell" guarantees a commission to the listed agent if the house is sold. For example, the owner produces a buyer who purchases the house. The agent is still entitled to his commission regardless of whether he contributed to the sale.

• Multiple listing. The owner lists the property with a single real estate agent. This agent places it in several agencies. The agent who produces a buyer must then split the commission with the single listed agent.

Much of the litigation concerning real estate agent contracts centers on the issue of what duties the agent must complete to earn his commission. In general, once the agent has produced a person who is "ready, willing and able" to purchase the home, he has earned his commission. If the owner then refuses to sell, it is possible that he still may have to pay the agent a commission. In another instance, suppose the owner has signed a listing contract for a ninety-day period. The agent brings Mr. and Mrs. Williams to see the home. They like the house but do not agree to buy it until after the listing contract expires. Since the agent produced the purchaser, he will be able to collect his commission although the sale took place after the expiration of the listing contract. Consequently, a property owner should clearly define the terms under which the real estate agent will receive his commission.

Generally, listings run for periods of thirty, sixty, or ninety days. This also should be clearly stated in the contract. In addition, some listing contracts are extended automatically unless the seller notifies the agent in writing ten days prior to the named termination date. The owner should read the listing contract carefully to see if an automatic extension clause is included in his contract. If so, he should be certain that he is aware of the proper means of notification. A notification of the owner's desire not to extend the listing should be sent by certified mail-return receipt requested. The receipt will serve as proof that the notification has been delivered to the agent.

Courts occasionally recognize the existence of an "oral contract" for a listing with a real estate agency. If the property owner does not wish to employ a real estate agent, he should refrain from giving the agency any impression that he would welcome its services. In many cases, if the agency procures a buyer, and it appears that the property owner's statements authorized this action, the owner may find that he owes the agent a commission.

The prospective buyer generally has little interest in the relationship between the agent and the property owner. In most cases, the agent is dependent only on the owner for his commission. Therefore, the individual who wishes to sell his property should be aware of his rights and liabilities in relation to listing contracts. With this knowledge, he can choose a real estate listing contract that best serves his needs.

Purchase contract

Many people believe that the major transaction in a real estate sale is the closing or settlement of the purchase. However, settlement is merely the final execution of the terms in the sales contract. All areas of disagreement should be settled while each side still retains some bargaining power. Once the contract is signed, both parties must abide by its terms.

From the buyer's point of view, the sales contract embodies all that he is purchasing. If an item is not listed in the contract, there is no definite assurance that he has a valid right to it at the time of the settlement. This is particularly true of items such as carpeting, curtain rods, kitchen appliances, and wall shelves. Once the owner and the prospective buyer agree on the items to be sold with the house, the buyer should be certain that these items are specifically mentioned in the sales contract. Even the preprinted forms leave room for inserting items of this nature.

The most important single item in the sales contract is the legal description of the property. Sometimes this description is transposed verbatim from the official county records. However, when the land is part of a modern subdivision, the sales contract and the deed will merely state a lot and section number and refer the reader to a record book in the county courthouse. As a cross-reference, it is advisable to include the street address as well as the legal description. For example:

> Lot 159, Section 260 of the Apple Orchard Subdivision, as platted and recorded in Deed Book 2442, among the land records of Any County, Anystate,

> U.S.A., and also known as 7720 Maple Street, Centertown, Anystate.

Occasionally a sales contract will describe the property solely by the house and street number. This is risky practice and should be avoided if at all possible.

A sales contract should also include the full names of both parties to the contract, the date, the selling price, and the terms of payment. Normally, the prospective buyer will make a down payment as "earnest money." This payment serves as evidence of his intention to purchase the home. Usually the contract also states that the buyer will forfeit his down payment if he fails to carry out the terms of the agreement. However, many contracts protect the buyer by making the purchase contingent upon the availability of satisfactory financing. This is often the case when the buyer is being financed by a VA or FHA loan which is guaranteed by the federal government. In this situation, the contract becomes null and void if the buyer cannot obtain proper financing. Furthermore, the buyer's deposit is returned to him.

Most contracts require the seller to provide the buyer with a "general warranty" deed. In this document, the seller guarantees that the buyer is receiving a good title to the land. The general warranty deed can be distinguished from the "quit claim" deed in which the seller merely relinquishes his rights to the property. There is no guarantee in the latter case that the seller has good title to the land.

Finally, the contract provides that all terms be carried out by a certain date or within a stated number of days, usually thirty to sixty days. This date is often referred to as the closing or settlement date. The contract also requires certain costs such as taxes, insurance, heating oil, etc., to be prorated as of the closing date. Also, the sale contract determines who bears such costs as transfer fees and state revenue stamps. In many instances these items are negotiable. The actual expense will be settled as a part of the closing costs. This discussion emphasizes the importance of the sales contract because it regulates the execution of all further acts. A clear understanding of possible pitfalls will help both buyer and seller determine whether the sales contract truly reflects the terms to which they have agreed.

Closing

The day on which the terms of the contract are executed is often referred to as the *closing* or *settlement*. The closing date is generally thirty to sixty days after the contract is signed and gathers together the buyer, the seller, their wives, and respective attorneys, if desired. At this time, the financing has been approved; the title examined; title insurance procured; and the deed has been prepared for execution and delivery.

The settlement is sometimes the occasion for the termination or creation of an *escrow*. Generally speaking, an *escrow* is an arrangement by which one party delivers a legal document or money into the keeping of a third person. This party holds the item until the advent of a certain condition; then delivers it to another party. For example, suppose at the time the sale contract was signed, the prospective buyer made a deposit of $5,000. The buyer wants assurance that his money will be returned if he does not obtain the necessary financing. He and the seller therefore agree to give the money to a third person, perhaps a bank, until the financing is approved. If the buyer gets his loan, the bank will apply the deposit toward the purchase price at the closing. In this instance, the closing would mark the termination of an escrow agreement.

An escrow can also be created on the settlement day. For instance, suppose Jones is purchasing Smith's house on an installment basis. Jones pays Smith a deposit of $5,000 and agrees to pay the balance of the purchase price over the next twenty years. The deed will be delivered to Jones upon the completion of the payments. In this situation, the deed to the land is delivered to an escrow. The holder of the deed is authorized to give it to the buyer when the entire purchase price has been paid. This prevents the seller from illegally conveying the deed to another person—an act which would create a title defect as well as protracted litigation. The escrow arrangement created at the closing would reasonably safeguard both buyer and seller.

The closing also presents an opportunity for final objections to any possible defects in the title. Often these defects are merely minor imperfections which can be corrected at the closing itself. Major defects usually are discovered and resolved during the title search.

An important document received by both buyer and seller at the closing is the "closing statement." Essentially an account, this document lists the itemized cost of the entire transaction. It indicates the adjustment of certain costs, such as the proration of taxes, insurance premiums, sewer service, the assumption of an existing mortgage, and the interest payments. Sometimes the attorneys in charge of the closing will send out the prepared closing statement in advance so that the buyer and seller can examine carefully the computations for the proration of the various costs.

The closing statement is the basis for computing the income tax for the year. Applicable deductions are shown on the statement. It is also the source for computation of depreciation if the property is rented out. Finally, it can be used to calculate the capital gain or loss for the seller and the cost basis for the buyer. In the latter case, the buyer uses this statement to determine his gain or loss when he resells the property. Thus, the closing statement should be maintained in a secure place, preferably a safe deposit box.

At the closing, the seller and his wife execute the deed and deliver it to the buyer and his wife. This is the formal transfer of ownership of the property. Of course, the sellers also transfer the keys to the home as well as other essentials. These include the names of utility companies and similar services.

The closing procedure generally lasts about an hour. Afterwards, the closer, who is usually the lender's representative, records the deed and mortgage in the county courthouse, procures the title insurance in the new owner's name, and mails these documents to the buyer. The seller receives his final payment from the closer after the documents have been recorded and the financing has been processed.

There are, of course, many other technical aspects relating to the purchase, sale, and ownership of real property, but a basic knowledge of applicable laws may help the reader deal with them.

Chapter Eleven

Making a Will and Planning an Estate

Every individual should carefully consider the merits of making a valid will. Too many people put off this task until it is too late. Unfortunately, death without a will often results in confusion, family arguments, and protracted legal battles.

Through a will the individual commands the disposition of his possessions. In the absence of a will, a person loses this power to command. It is left to others, notably the courts, to dispose of the individual's possessions. This is done according to the distribution structure established by state law. Thus, by failing to make a will, the individual may unwittingly injure his family and friends.

A "will" is a written document by which the testator (maker of the will) provides for the disposition of his property, both real and personal. A will takes legal effect only at the date of death. Until that time, the person can revoke his original will, leaving no will; he can amend his will; or he can destroy it and make a new one.

At one time or another, most people reflect on the advisibility of making a will. Since individual circumstances differ widely, the reasons people choose to make wills also differ. However, few can conceive of a situation in which a person is not advised to make a will. Take this example:

> John and Mary Smith are of moderate means. They have two children. They rent a modest apartment and own a second-hand car valued at about $1,000. Their joint checking account contains about $1,500. In addition, John has a $20,000 life insurance policy in which he names Mary as the beneficiary. John's only other personal property is the furniture in the apartment and $4,000 which he has saved in a joint account. His entire "estate" totals no more than $30,000, while $60,000 is the minimum for which federal estate tax returns must be filed.

Should John have a will? Certainly he does not have to worry about saving taxes. He would have to double his net worth before needing to file a federal estate return. Therefore, a common reason for making a will—to save estate taxes—would not apply in this situation.

Many people make wills to avoid having their property distributed against their wishes—in other words, according to the impersonal laws of intestate (dying without a will) distribution. This reason is valid and should be considered seriously in evaluating whether a personal situation requires a will. However, in John's situation, the law would most likely give one-third of the property to his wife and two-thirds to his children. Furthermore, the car, the checking account, and the savings are all owned jointly. This property would not be a part of the probate estate. As the surviving owner, Mary Smith would retain these items. The life insurance policy specifies Mary as the sole beneficiary. Consequently, it would not pass through probate. She would receive the entire amount without needless administrative delay. Thus, if John died without a will, it would be no different than if he died with a will which left everything to his wife.

There are, however, two important reasons for having a will besides saving taxes and avoiding the impersonal disposition of property by the state. For example, suppose John and Mary died in the same accident. Most likely all the property would be thrown into probate. In the absence of a will, the court would be required to distribute the assets according to the scheme set out by that state's statutes. This disposition may not be in accordance with John's wishes.

Most likely the assets of John's estate would be placed in a cumbersome guardianship for the benefit of his children. A guardianship can be expensive, inflexible, and unnecessary, whereas, if John made a will, he could provide for this contingency. Of course, the laws of the state in which the will is probated dictate who can be chosen as a trustee or guardian. The person named in the will must meet the state's qualifications of competency. In general, however, the trust provides a more flexible, less expensive and more workable arrangement for the management of funds during the children's minority.

For example, John's children might be raised outside of the state in which the estate was probated. A trust in the will could work out any conflicts of law in advance. On the other hand, an in-state guardianship may be hampered by procedures made archaic by the mobility of today's population. Thus, through his will, John can plan for the management of his estate should he and his wife die before their children attain adulthood.

If John and Mary were to die at the same time, someone would have to take care of the children. This would be a guardian of their persons, whereas the guardianship discussed in the preceding paragraph provides for the management of the estate until the children reach majority. The two positions are not necessarily held by the same individual. For example, a bank might manage the funds, while the decedent's brother might be chosen as the guardian of the children. As in the case of the trustee, the personal guardian also must meet the requirements of state law.

Still the authority to designate a guardian and a trustee is a powerful reason for making a will. If there is no will, the court will appoint someone to care for the children.

Thus, the example of John and Mary Smith illustrates that even young people who are not wealthy, who have no fear of estate taxes, and who have everything in joint survivorship accounts are fully protected only if they have a will.

Despite these arguments, many people continue to doubt the need for a will. They insist that the chance of husband and wife dying at the same time is remote. This may be true when based on national statistics. However, when deaths occur, they happen to individuals, not statistics. Thus, the individuals should take proper precautions. When the small effort and cost of preparing a will is weighed against the uncertainties and probable confusion caused by having the situation thrown into an impersonal court, it is easy to see why making a will *now* is important for every individual, no matter what his age or station in life.

When there is no will

A person who dies without a valid will is said to have died "intestate." Every state has laws of "intestate succession" which prescribe the disposition of a person's estate when he dies without a will. In effect, the state government writes a will for him. His real property is distributed according to the laws of the state in which it is located. His personal property is distributed according to the laws of the state in which he was residing at the time of death.

The laws of the various states differ widely as to the quantity of the estate awarded to the surviving spouse and to the children. It is impossible to cover the rules of all the states in one short chapter. An example of one state, however, will illustrate the principles involved, as well as providing a general idea of the situation in other states.

Assume a married man owns a home worth $30,000, and has personal property totaling $15,000. If he dies without a will, the laws of the state of Michigan provide for the following disposition of his property:

a. *If children.* If he leaves surviving children, in addition to his wife, the state grants the wife one-third of the real estate ($10,000). The children inherit two-thirds of the real estate ($20,000). If he leaves more than one child, the children receive rights to two-thirds of the personal property ($10,000). The wife receives the remaining one-third ($5,000). If the decedent leaves only one child, that child would inherit one-half of the personal property ($7,500). The surviving wife also would receive one-half ($7,500).

b. *No children.* If the decedent died, leaving only his wife, the state would allow her to inherit one-half of the real estate ($15,000). The remaining one-half would be inherited by the decedent's parents, brothers, sisters, or the children of any deceased brothers and sisters. If none of these relatives is alive, the wife inherits the entire real estate.

As to personal property, if the decedent dies and any of the persons mentioned above are alive, the law states that the surviving wife inherits all of the personal property if it totals $3,000 or less. If it exceeds this amount, she inherits one-half of the rest. In this example, she would receive $3,000 plus one-half of $12,000 ($15,000—3,000), or a total of $9,000. If none of the relatives mentioned in the preceding paragraph are alive, the surviving wife inherits all of the personal property.

This example serves to disprove one common fallacy. When a man dies without a will, the state does not take a major share of his property. It is only when the decedent leaves neither a wife, children, grandchildren, parents, brothers, sisters, grandparents, or children of these relatives, that the state claims the property. This forfeiture is termed "escheat." In other words, the property escheats to the state government.

The preceding example also illustrates another important point. If a man dies without a will, he has absolutely no control over the distribution of *his* property. It will be distributed impersonally, solely in accordance with state law. It may well happen that his surviving spouse receives inadequate support while relatives for whom he cares little gain windfall inheritances.

Also, this example describes only one state's laws of intestate succession. The laws in your own state may effect a different result, since the rules governing distribution of an estate vary widely from state to state. Generally, however, these laws tend to favor the surviving spouse and children. Furthermore, many states tend to favor the children over the surviving spouse.

State laws specifically differ over the share of the estate to be granted to the decedent's grandchildren. The following example illustrates this situation:

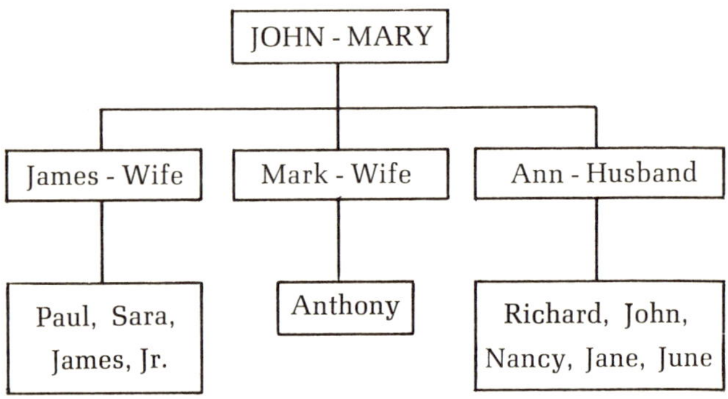

Assume that John and Mary have three children, James, Mark, and Ann. Each one marries and bears children, as indicated in the diagram. John is the principal character since it is the distribution of his estate with which we are concerned. His estate consists of $30,000 in real estate and $15,000 in personal property, a total of $45,000. John's wife and all three of their immediate children (James, Mark, and Ann) are already deceased. Thus, according to general principles of law, when John dies, his grandchildren will receive the entire estate. The important question, over which the states differ, is the *amount* each grandchild will receive.

Some states distribute the inheritance *per stirpes*, meaning by roots or by representation through the immediate parents. In other words, this method of distribution would grant equal shares to the three branches (James, Mark, and Ann) of John's estate. Each branch would be entitled to one-third of the estate, or $15,000. Under this method of distribution, Anthony, being the only child of Mark's branch of the family, would receive the entire $15,000. On the other hand, Ann's branch share of $15,000 would be divided among her five children. Each of these grandchildren would receive $3,000. Other states provide that the children inherit *per capita* or according to the number of individuals of equal degrees of descent. This method of distribution provides equal shares for each of John's grandchildren because they all stand in the same degree of descent. Thus, if the total estate of $45,000 were distributed *per capita,* it would be equally divided among the nine grandchildren. Each individual would receive $5,000.

Effect of having a will

There are many advantages that result from starting and maintaining an up-to-date will:

• You can be sure that the property in your estate will be distributed according to your desires.

• You can appoint your own executor.

• You can select the guardian who will care for any surviving minor children.

• You can minimize certain costs of the estate. For example, you can specify that the executor does not have to post bond to insure the faithful performance of his duties.

• You can arrange for cash to be made available to pay debts and provide for necessary expenses.

• You can name charities which you wish to help.

• You can specify the amount that each beneficiary will receive. This provides immeasurable flexibility from the rigid rules governing a state's formula for intestate distribution.

• You can select the method by which minor children receive their bequests. This includes the naming of a guardian for the funds of the minor, and the designation of the number and type of restrictions to be imposed on the management of the funds. If the testator so desires, he can relieve the guardian of his duty to submit an annual accounting of the principle and income of the fund. This requirement is usually imposed in the absence of a clear direction to the contrary.

Types of wills

Holographic will. This term describes a will which is written entirely in the handwriting of the testator. A holographic will is null and void in a majority of states. It is interesting to note that a famous columnist, the late Drew Pearson, left a number of wills when he died. One of the contested documents was a holographic will which he had written by hand on the stationery of a Louisville hotel almost forty years ago.

Nuncupative will. This is an oral will. Many states hold that a nuncupative will is null and void. Other states uphold its validity in certain situations. For example, in the state of California, an individual in the military who is actually in the field or at sea can make a valid nuncupative will. However, at the time he makes the oral will, the individual must be in actual fear of death or in expectation of receiving injuries that same day. In addition, the will must be witnessed by two persons, and the person making the will must request one of them to bear witness to the fact that his statement is his will. Furthermore, the State of California limits the disposition of property to personal property totaling no more than $1,000. Procedurally, the will must be written down within thirty days and offered for probate within six months of the person's death.

Joint wills and mutual wills. A single will executed by two or more persons is known as a joint will. It must be offered for probate when each of the signers dies. A joint will is cumbersome since it is a single instrument that binds two or more persons to its terms. One of its chief disadvantages is that once the first signer dies, the remaining persons may not be able to revoke or amend the terms of the will. However, this may be overcome by a contrary provision in the will.

Mutual wills have reciprocal provisions. In general, they are executed by man and wife. Usually, the husband leaves everything to his wife, and the wife leaves everything to her husband. Other contingency bequests are the same in each will.

In the case of a joint will, many states automatically presume that it was executed pursuant to an agreement and, therefore, prevent the survivors from revoking or amending its terms. Some states apply the same terms to mutual wills. The state may presume that the mutual wills were executed according to an agreement governing the particular disposition of the property. Thus, once one of the parties dies, the other is bound by the contract not to revoke his or her will. However, this presumption may not be applied as strongly to a case of mutual wills as to a joint will.

Conditional will. This term describes a written document which becomes a valid will in the event of a certain happening. There are many legal pitfalls in this area. Thus, it is best to avoid the problem by executing a more conventional will. However, if an individual wishes to make a conditional will, he should state, clearly and expressly, the condition which must be fulfilled in order to make the will operative.

Formal requirements for the execution of a will

A will should insure that a person's wishes will be carried out after death. Thus, it is best to prepare a conventional document that will stand up in court. Each state lists certain formal requirements for the execution of a valid will. For example, according to California statutes a valid will must contain the following elements:

- Anyone over 18 years of age and of sound mind can dispose of property by a will.
- A will must be in writing. It must be signed by the testator and acknowledged by him as his will.

• The signing of the will must take place in the presence of two witnesses who also must sign and attest to the fact that they witnessed the signing.

In addition, state law may prescribe the form and place of the signature. For example:

> The foregoing instrument, consisting of ___ pages, including the page signed by the testator, was at the date hereof, by the said (John Smith, testator), signed, sealed, published, and declared to be his last will in the presence of us, who at his request, and in his presence, and in the presence of each other, have signed the same as witnesses hereto.
>
> Date
>
> ____________________ Residing at ____________________
>
> ____________________ Residing at ____________________

Usually, the will is signed in the attorney's office. For example, John Smith wishes to make a will. He makes several preliminary trips to his lawyer to discuss the ultimate disposition of his property. The lawyer draws up a rough draft which John reads over. If John has any questions or desired changes, he and his lawyer can clarify the problem areas. Once the content is set, the lawyer will have the will typed again and set up an appointment for its formal execution. At the appointed hour, John Smith will come to the attorney's conference room. The lawyer will bring in two disinterested persons to act as witnesses to the will. These people may well be fellow lawyers in the building or other impartial persons who are willing to witness John Smith's execution of his will. When they are assembled, John Smith will read the will over, acknowledge that it is his will, and ask the two people if they will witness his signature to the will. After the testator has signed the will, one of the witnesses reads aloud the formal paragraph quoted above. Then each of the witnesses signs, giving his present residence and the date of execution. In less than five minutes, John Smith has executed his will and stands fully protected and assured that the post-mortem distribution of his estate will be in accordance with his expressed desire.

Subsequent changes of a will

A valid will is not irrevocable. The individual can amend it, change it, or simply revoke it and become "will-less" again. The conditions for any subsequent changes in a person's will are approximately the same as those required for the initial execution of the will.

A "codicil" is an amendment to a will. It may add to the will's provisions. Suppose Smith becomes the owner of a large art collection. Since this acquisition occurred after the execution of the will, there is no mention of the art collection in that document. To insure that it will be handled as he desires, Smith should add a "codicil" that refers solely to the disposition of the art collection. A codicil must be executed in the same manner as the formal execution of the original will.

Some jurisdictions also provide for "revocation by circumstances." For example, Smith, a bachelor, executes a will and leaves his entire estate to his girlfriend, Raquel. Later, he breaks up with Raquel, dates Mary, and finally marries her. However, he never reviewed his will and consequently died without rewriting it. Thus Smith purportedly left everything to Raquel. Under these circumstances the law will imply a revocation because the legal presumption is that Smith would not intend to benefit Raquel through his will. Smith's estate would be distributed under the laws of intestate succession, as if he had died without leaving a will.

A testator also can "partially revoke" his will. This is a properly executed document which revokes certain parts of the will and leaves others intact. However, this document must be extremely clear as to which clauses of the will it intends to revoke. As long as the document provides a clear expression of the testator's intent the law will give it legal effect.

Just as a will can be amended, so also can it be revoked. When a will is revoked, its legal effect is nullified. Each state has express provisions governing the revocation of a will.

For example, Illinois holds that an otherwise valid will is revoked by any of the following acts:

- The testator can revoke his will by burning, tearing, or otherwise obliterating it. He can also direct another person to destroy it. However, accidentally burning part of the will does not constitute a revocation because there is no intent to destroy the will. The intent without the act, or the act without the intent, is insufficient to revoke a will. Both must be present.
- The execution of another will which expressly states that the prior will is hereby revoked.
- The execution of a later will which is inconsistent with and which fails to mention the former will.
- The execution of a separate document which declares the will to be revoked. The signing of this document must include the same formalities as the signing of the first will.

Estate planning

Most Americans make wills to insure that their property is distributed according to their wishes and to provide for the proper physical care of their children. Those persons whose net worth is in excess of $60,000, the minimum estate upon which a federal estate tax can be imposed, have another important reason for making a will. Through this document they can save costs in estate administration and estate taxes. Because of the progressive tax rate on the dollar value of an estate, the importance of sound planning increases with the level of a person's net worth. The experts in the field refer to this foresight as "estate planning."

Individual problems can best be solved by seeking individual advice that takes into full account the myriad possibilities of action and the legal precedents and theories supporting one's plan. Good sound business judgment also weighs heavily in determining the proper course of action. Subsequent illustrations suggest various possibilities which may be useful in a particular situation.

As mentioned earlier, everyone receives an automatic exemption of $60,000. Thus, a person with a $60,000 estate pays no taxes. In an estate of $70,000, only $10,000 would be taxable. The federal estate tax rises steeply. It ranges from 3 percent on the first $5,000 of the "taxable estate" to 77 percent on amounts of $10,000,000 and more. A taxable estate is the gross estate less all valid deductions and exemptions. As inferred, the determination of the "gross estate" has an important impact on the amount of taxes which must ultimately be paid. It includes all property, real and personal, tangible and intangible. This list may include houses, furnishings, life insurance policies, stocks, bonds, books, business interests, cars, and other interests upon which some value can be placed. The gross estate is decreased by the amount of all permissible deductions and exemptions. This leaves the "taxable estate." A person can reduce his taxable estate by excluding property from his gross estate, or by insuring that the property is deductible from the gross estate under current estate tax laws.

Marital deduction. The marital deduction was enacted into the federal estate tax laws in 1948. It permits a husband or wife to give his/her spouse up to one-half of the adjusted gross estate. This amount is deducted from the adjusted gross estate in order to arrive at the taxable estate.

The marital deduction was enacted to give equal opportunities for tax savings to people in states that do not have community property laws. According to the laws of community property each marriage partner owns one-half of all property earned or accumulated by the other from the date of marriage until the death of one of the parties. Under these laws, when the husband or wife died, only one-half of the "community property" is subject to federal estate taxes. States that have community property laws include

California, Texas, Arizona, Idaho, Louisiana, New Mexico, Nevada, and Washington.

However, by using the marital deduction, anyone can achieve these same results, thereby avoiding double taxation of the property. Thus, if there was no marital deduction, all property would be taxed at the death of the husband in those states without community property laws. Then, if it was bequeathed to the wife, it would be taxed again as part of her estate.

The marital deduction does not apply if the decedent's gross estate consists exclusively of property held by the decedent and his surviving spouse as community property under the law of his state. Thus, no person can take advantage of both the community property laws and the marital deduction.

A simple illustration will demonstrate the importance of this deduction. Baker has a gross estate valued at $130,000, which he leaves entirely to his wife. One-half of the gross estate would mean a marital deduction of $65,000. The remaining amount is decreased further by the estate tax exemption of $60,000. This leaves a taxable estate of only $5,000. The applicable tax rate for $5,000 is 3 percent. The total federal estate tax is only $150.

Consider also the case of someone more affluent: Able dies and leaves a gross estate of $500,000. He leaves $300,000 to his wife and the rest to other relatives. The application of the marital deduction will reduce the gross estate by one-half, from $500,000 to $250,000. As we have seen, the estate tax laws permit the marital deduction to include only one-half of the adjusted gross estate. Therefore, Able's wife can deduct only $250,000 of her $300,000 inheritance. The estate tax exemption of $60,000 further decreases Able's taxable estate. Thus, federal estate tax will have to be paid on $190,000.

When Able's wife dies, the $300,000 which she inherited from her husband will be included in her gross estate. Assume that amount to be the total value of her gross estate. Since the marital deduction has already been applied

Alternative Tax Estimates

	Use of marital deduction		Not using marital deduction
	Able	Able's wife	Able
Gross estate	$500,000	$300,000	$500,000
Marital deduction	250,000	—	—
Adjusted estate	250,000	300,000	500,000
Exemption	60,000	60,000	60,000
Taxable estate	190,000	240,000	440,000
Tax	47,700 +	62,700	126,500
Total tax	$110,400		$126,500

Savings $16,100

to that property and since the husband is already dead, the marital deduction cannot be applied again. However, the usual $60,000 exemption will be applied to her estate. Thus, the taxable estate left by Able's wife is $240,000.

There is another subtle advantage in lowering estate taxes by using the marital deduction. Because the tax is a progressive tax, it is best to apply the taxes to two estates, the husband's and the wife's, rather than to one large estate. Thus, in our example, the tax on Able's estate of $190,000 would be $20,700 + 30 percent of $90,000 or a total tax of $47,700. On his wife's taxable estate of $240,000 the tax would be $20,700 + 30 percent of $140,000 or a total tax of $62,700.

These amounts seem high. However, when compared to the tax that would have been imposed on Able's original estate of $500,000, they represent an appreciable savings. For example, if Able's original gross estate of $500,000 had remained intact, the only allowable exemption would be $60,000, leaving a taxable estate of $440,000. The estate tax imposed on this amount would be ($65,700 + 32 percent of $190,000), or a tax of $126,500. Compare this figure with the sums of the two estate taxes on the two estates resulting from the marital deduction: $47,700 + $62,700 = $110,400. The tax savings resulting from the marital deduction total $16,100. Furthermore, as the size of the estate increases, the savings in estate taxes through the marital deduction also increase.

One of the most important limitations on the marital deduction is that the property must "qualify" in order to be included. Life insurance proceeds, although perhaps not a part of the probate estate, may qualify for the marital deduction. Other types of property may be willed with certain restrictions.

For example, a husband gives his wife a restricted power of appointment. At her death she appoints one of his grandchildren to be the recipient of a certain piece of property. Property willed to a spouse qualifies for the marital deduction only if the recipient of the property has complete power to save, spend or dispose of the property as he or she desires. In our earlier example, the power of appointment would not "qualify" for the marital deduction, since it is not a general power.

In another case, suppose the decedent bequeathed a tract of land to his wife for twenty years, with a provision that the land should thereafter be given to a third party. The value of that tract of land would not qualify as part of the marital deduction because the spouse did not have complete ownership over the property. Instead, she had a "terminable interest" or an interest in the land which would expire at the end of twenty years. Thus, she did not have complete power to spend or dispose of the property. She was bound by the twenty-year provision.

Life insurance. Life insurance policies also can be used to reduce estate taxes. Farsighted planning not only avoids cumbersome procedures, it also saves important tax dollars.

Proceeds from life insurance can be excluded from the "probate estate" yet still remain part of the federal "taxable estate" of a decedent. The life insurance proceeds are excluded from the probate estate when the holder of the policy names a person as the beneficiary. Generally, the only time a policy is included in the *probate* estate is when the beneficiary is designated as "my estate." Excluding a life insurance policy from the proceeds of the probate estate provides liquidity. It allows the beneficiary of the policy to collect the money without waiting until the probate court approves the distribution of the estate's assets.

To reduce taxes, however, the life insurance proceeds must be excluded from the "taxable estate." According to the federal tax laws the life insurance proceeds while excluded from probate are still part of the taxable estate if the decedent has retained the "incidents of ownership." This means that he has kept the right to change beneficiaries, the right to borrow against the cash value of the policy, the right to assign or regain full ownership of the policy, and the right to select settlement options under the terms of the policy. However, if the individual relinquishes these incidents of ownership to another person, the proceeds of the life insurance policy will be excluded from his gross estate. Exclusion of this money can mean significant reductions in estate taxes.

Many workers in the United States work for corporations or companies that have established fringe benefits such as pensions, health insurance, disability pay, and group term life insurance. The income tax laws of the United States permit an employer to provide up to $50,000 in group term life insurance protection and to deduct the cost from the company's income as a legitimate business deduction.

Under certain circumstances, the employe can use this life insurance to his further advantage by employing a little foresight. The Internal Revenue has ruled, Revenue Ruling 68-334, that the employe can give the incidents of ownership in his group life insurance policy to his family, thereby keeping the policy proceeds out of his taxable estate. This means up to an additional $50,000 can be excluded from the taxable estate. Again, this results in significant savings in estate taxes.

However, the government places two prequisites on this assignment of group policies:

- *Both* the group policy and the relevant state law must permit the employe to give away all his incidents of ownership in the policy, including the privilege of converting the group term insurance into a permanent life policy if he leaves the company's employment.
- The assignment must be irrevocable.

This ruling provides a potentially important estate planning tool, but it is a very technical area of tax law. It should not be exercised without considerable thought and professional advice. Furthermore, circumstances can change. Suppose, the employe wishes to change the beneficiary, or the beneficiary dies before the policy holder. Relinquishing ownership rights to the policy abolishes the policy holder's ability to act. On the other hand, if circumstances permit, assigning the policy to another person can exclude large sums of money from the taxable estate and result in substantial savings.

Gifts. Informed and judicious gift-giving can also reduce the taxable estate. Lifetime giving is perhaps the simplest way to reduce estate taxes. Some people contend that the gift tax is as oppressive as the estate tax. However, statistics reveal that the gift tax is only about three-fourths as much as the estate tax on the same property. In addition, some important exemptions and exclusions further enhance the tax advantages of lifetime giving.

Intra-family gifts have long been utilized to reduce estate taxes. The limits on this practice are the lifetime exemption and the annual exclusion of gifts. Every person is entitled to a lifetime exemption of $30,000 in tax-free gifts. A married couple can collect up to $60,000 in tax-free gifts. Thus, an individual can give away up to $30,000, either all at once or in separate parcels and not have any gift tax imposed upon him. Thus, if Baker gives Jones $30,000 in stock, there is no gift tax because Baker can avail himself of the gift tax exemption. The $30,000 *exemption* can only be used once. However, it need not be used all at once. Thus, Baker could grant Jones $10,000 one year, Smith, $10,000 another year, and Williams $10,000 the third year. Furthermore, if Baker is married, he and his wife can "split" their gifts and give away tax-free amounts totaling $60,000.

In addition to the $30,000 exemption, there is a $3,000 annual *exclusion* for each donee. An individual can give up to $3,000 annually to as many persons as he wishes without paying any gift tax. Thus, if Baker gave $3,000 each to Jones, Smith, and Williams, the following year he still would not pay any gift tax because all of his gifts that year were within the $3,000 annual exclusion. The annual exclusion is also subject to split giving. Thus, Baker and his wife can give up to $6,000 per year per donee without incurring any gift tax.

One can readily appreciate the appealing aspects, from an estate tax point of view, of lifetime giving. There are also bad points. It is naturally human for people to want to keep their possessions as long as possible. Accordingly, most people are reluctant to take full advantage of lifetime giving. Also, most people want to be financially protected for their entire life. If a person lives a long life, he will need substantial sums to maintain his home and provide for any physical care that might be required. If the individual gives everything away, he may be powerless to insure his own self-sufficiency—an unhappy result if he has worked his entire life to accumulate a sum on which to retire.

Bequeathing charitable gifts, in one's will is another

important method of reducing estate taxes. This "giving after death" results in the deduction of the full amount of the charitable bequest. Suppose Baker has a gross estate of $500,000. He can leave one-half of that amount to his wife and reduce his taxes by the marital deduction. If he gives the other half to charity, that amount is also deductible as a charitable bequest. His taxable estate is zero. Thus, the marital deduction and the charitable bequest can be combined to eliminate the estate tax entirely, no matter what the size of the estate. However, there are certain disadvantages to this method of avoiding taxes. One-half of the entire estate is gone. In many cases, the individual may prefer to give that half of his estate to his family and sustain the estate taxes. This method would at least accumulate additional wealth in the family.

One tax provision, which sometimes catches the donor unaware, is the taxation of "gifts in contemplation of death." According to this rule, if a person makes a gift within three years of his death, he is presumed to have made that gift in contemplation of death. The inference is that he gave the gift to avoid estate taxes. If a gift is within this category, its value must be included in the gross estate, and federal estate taxes must be paid on it. This is important because the federal estate tax rate is substantially higher than the gift tax rate.

If the executor of the estate can establish that the deceased did not expect to die within the next three years, the gift will be excluded from the taxable estate. To illustrate, suppose Baker makes a gift at age seventy. If he then dies at age seventy-two, it will be difficult to establish that he was not thinking of dying at that age. However, if Baker makes the gift at the age of thirty-nine and dies one year later in a sudden automobile accident, the executor should succeed in establishing that the gift was a *bona fide* gift and not made in contemplation of death.

Jointly owned property. Jointly owned property passes to the survivor without going through a will or the probate administrative process. Nevertheless it is subject to fed-

eral estate taxes to the extent that the person whose estate is involved contributed to the purchase price of the property. The government presumes for estate tax purposes that the first joint owner to die contributed the entire purchase price, in the case of real property, or the entire amount of money in a joint bank account. If the survivor contributed any of the money, she can rebut the government's presumption by presenting appropriate evidence. If the survivor succeeds in proving that he contributed some money, that amount will not be included in the gross estate. No taxes will be collected on it at this point.

Trusts. A revocable lifetime trust can be changed or amended during the maker's lifetime. Accordingly it is subject to federal estate taxes when the person who established the trust dies. An irrevocable trust cannot be changed or amended during the life of the maker. However, it may be subject to the estate tax if the person who set it up derived any benefits from it, or if he retained the right to alter any terms of the trust. A testamentary trust is established by the terms of a will. As such it is part of the decedent's estate and is subject to estate taxes.

Sensible estate planning can mean substantial savings for those who inherit your property. However, this planning is not simple mechanics. It involves a thorough inventory of your present and future resources and a compelling desire to see your property distributed according to your own wishes.

Chapter Twelve

Probate and Handling an Estate

It has often been said that the only two certainties of life are death and taxes. Both of these certainties are involved in estate administration. When an individual dies, his estate is subject to federal and state tax laws. An "estate" consists of everything a man owns at the time of his death. This includes both real and personal property. Whether or not a person has a will does not materially affect the estate's administration. All estates are subject to a formal legal procedure which approves the distribution of the contents of the estate. This procedure is usually called *probate,* and the court is known as the probate court, the surrogate's court, or orphan's court.

The term "probate" is derived from Latin and means "to prove." Thus, it applies to the process of proving the validity of the decedent's will. When its validity has been proven, the will becomes a matter of public record. The probate court will then supervise the administration of the estate and approve its final distribution. If there is no will, the contents of the estate will be distributed according to the laws of the state. Again, the probate court will supervise the administration of the estate and will approve the final distribution.

A discussion of estate administration can be divided into

five general areas:

- Administering an estate
- Gathering of all assets and information
- Managing the estate
- Determining claims, debts, and paying taxes
- Distributing the assets of the estate

Who administers the estate

When an estate is processed through the probate court, someone must be in charge to insure that all obligations are fulfilled. It is this person's task to see that all people who are entitled to be paid are paid, to see that all people who owe money pay their just debts, and to make sure that the contents of the estate are distributed according to the desires of the decedent or according to law.

In law, the person who administers the estate is known by a number of titles. In general, he can be referred to as the personal representative of the decedent. If the decedent has named a specific individual in his will, that person is known as the *executor*. If the person named is a woman, she is called an *executrix*. In addition to administering the estate, the executor is obliged to carry out the terms of the will and to distribute the contents of the estate according to the manner specified in the decedent's will.

If the decedent did not leave a will, the probate court names an *administrator* to administer the estate. The administrator must process the estate and distribute its contents in accordance with state law. If the person named by the court is a woman, she is called an *administratrix*.

Although they are rarely applied, there are two other terms used to describe the administrator of an estate. If the person who was named executor by the decedent has already died or for some reason does not qualify, the probate court will name an *administrator cum testamento annexo*. This term describes an administrator who has a valid will attached. He must execute the terms of that will. For example, Donaldson makes a will in 1949 naming Johnson to be his executor. Johnson dies in 1958. Donaldson neglects to update his will. He dies in 1967 leaving the will as it was written in 1949. Since Johnson is dead, the probate court must name a substitute. This individual is technically called an *administrator cum testamento annexo.* In practice, his functions are the same as those of any other personal representative.

Another legal title is *administrator de bonis non cum testamento annexo.* This lengthy Latin phrase refers to an administrator who is appointed to complete the duties of a personal representative after they have been started by someone else. To illustrate, suppose Baker's will names Charles as the executor. While administering the estate, Charles dies of a sudden heart attack. The probate court must name someone to complete the administration and probate of Baker's estate. The person who is appointed to finish this job is called an *administrator de bonis non cum testamento annexo.*

When the decedent leaves a will which names an executor, there is usually no doubt who will administer the estate. The named executor will. The only exception to this rule occurs when the named executor is considered incompetent by the laws of that state.

For example, New York state law describes five classes of persons who are incompetent to be executors although they may have been named in the will. These include:

1. Persons under 21 years of age.

2. A person ruled incompetent or insane by a court of law.

3. Persons convicted of a felony (a serious crime).

4. Persons who are nonresident aliens. This clause refers to people living outside the state of New York who are not citizens of the United States.

5. Persons who are denied permission to administer an estate because they are unqualified. Under this provision, the court may refuse to grant a named executor permission to administer an estate if he is alcoholic, dishonest, or unable to read or write.

For example, suppose John Smith had been convicted of robbery. Mullen later appoints him executor of his estate. New York State would not allow Smith to assume this task because he had been convicted of a felony.

The laws of the various states differ widely over the conditions that preclude a person from acting as an administrator. For example, Illinois requires that a male executor be twenty-one whereas a woman can administer an estate at the age of eighteen. Illinois also refuses to allow anyone who is not a resident to be an administrator of an estate that is being probated in Illinois. However, a non-resident can be an executor, if named in the will.

If the probate court determines that the person named in the will is competent to act as an executor, the court usually accedes to the wishes of the decedent and formally approves that person. Accordingly, the probate court will issue an official document, usually called *letters testamentary*, which formally states that the person named is authorized to administer the estate.

If the decedent died without a will, the situation is more complicated. Since there is no will, there is no executor. Therefore the law must choose a person to administer the decedent's estate. Statutes in the individual states set up rigid procedures for the selection of the administrator or administratrix. (Once the personal representative is named, this book will refer to him as an administrator, even though his official title may be that of executor or some other technical legal name.)

The state of Illinois sets up a list of persons who are accorded preferential treatment in the probate court's appointment of an administrator. The order is as follows:

1. Surviving spouse
2. Children
3. Grandchildren
4. Father and mother
5. Brothers and sisters
6. Next of kin
7. Public administrator

8. Creditors

Thus, suppose Sam Olson died without a will. In admitting his estate to probate, the court will appoint his surviving wife to be the administratrix. If she is dead, and he has no children or grandchildren, the court will appoint Sam's father to administer the estate through probate. Other states have different laws. However, most states generally follow the above order of preferences, at least through the first six classes.

It is important to remember that the same rules for competency apply to persons appointed when there is no will as apply when an executor is named by a will. Both are subject to formal approval by the probate court. To illustrate this situation:

> Jones dies without having made a will. Normally, following the Illinois law, the probate court would appoint his wife to administer the estate. However, his wife is under eighteen. The court cannot name her because she is incompetent, or legally ineligible, to act as an administrator for the estate.

The court will have to seek further in its preferences until it finds a person who is competent to act as administrator. When the court finds someone who is in the preferred order and is competent, it will formally appoint that person as administrator.

Once the probate court has formally named an executor or administrator, it will issue a formal notice to that effect. This notice, known as letters testamentary or letters of administration, grants the administrator the necessary power to act on behalf of the estate and to carry out the orderly and proper administration of the estate.

Gathering of assets and information

Once an administrator has been appointed, he becomes the legal representative of the estate. He is expected to exercise the powers of his position in an honest, careful, and vigilant manner. Furthermore, the probate court administers a solemn oath to the administrator who must swear to perform his duties faithfully.

Many states also require that the administrator post bond. This procedure protects the decedent's creditors from any administrative mismanagement which might harm the creditor's claim. Generally, the bond is the amount of personal property in the estate plus an amount equal to two years' rents of the real property. Thus, if the value of the decedent's personal property is $15,000, and the yearly rent from his land totals $2,400 per year, the administrator would be required to post a bond of $19,800. Some states permit an administrator to perform his duties without posting a bond, if the testator expressly states in his will that no bond is to be posted. Other states will require the administrator to post the bond despite a will's express direction to the contrary.

After the will is filed with the court, the administrator must make an inventory of the estate. This involves listing all the property, both real and personal, owned by the decedent at the time of his death. He also should obtain the current addresses of the beneficiaries named in the will and learn whether any of them is a minor. If there is no will, the administrator should gather the names and addresses of the heirs-at-law.

The administrator's next function, in conjunction with the attorney, is to insure that a publication of death is inserted in the newspapers. The purpose of this insertion is to inform the creditors of the death and of the necessity of filing any claims against the decedent on or before a certain day. Generally, these death notices must be published once a week for three successive weeks prior to the final date for filing claims. With certain minor modifications, most published inserts follow this general form:

JONES, John J. Deceased
Smith and Smith, 300 Fourth Street, N.W., Attorneys
United States District Court for
the District of Columbia. Holding Probate Court.
No. 302-69, Administration.

> This is to give notice that the subscriber, of the District of Columbia, has obtained from the Probate Court of the District of Columbia, Letters Testamentary on the estate of John J. Jones, late of the District of Columbia, deceased. All persons having claims against the deceased are hereby warned to exhibit the same, with the vouchers thereof, legally authenticated, to the subscriber, on or before the 16th day of December, A.D. 1969; otherwise they may by law be excluded from all benefit of said estate. Given under my hand this 16th day of June 1969. CHARLES BAKER, 500 Maple Street, N.W. Attest: CAROL OLSON, Deputy Register of Wills for the District of Columbia, Clerk of the Probate Court.
>
> [Seal.] June 24, July 1, 8.

The next important function of the administrator is to inventory the contents of the safe deposit box, if one exists. Many states require a strict procedure for entry into a safe deposit box. For example, some states require that the administrator actually bring his letters of administration when he comes to inventory the contents of the box. States with inheritance taxes often require a state tax agent to be present at the opening. The reason for these state laws is to reduce the chances of fraud. For instance, someone might withhold certain items, such as cash or unregistered bonds.

To insure that accurate records of inheritance and transfer are maintained, many states that do not provide for the presence of a tax official, still require that someone be there to attest to the actual contents of the safe deposit box. The administrator's best course of action is to take several disinterested people with him, to list everything contained in the box, and then to have every person sign the list. Furthermore, it should be clearly indicated that the list contains everything found in the safe deposit box.

Finally, if the safe deposit box was jointly held by the decedent and another person, such as the surviving spouse, the administrator must consider the rights of the survivor with respect to the ownership and control of the contents of the safe deposit box. It may be necessary to obtain the survivor's consent before the box can be opened.

The administrator also must compile an inventory of any stocks, bonds or cash which were not in the safe deposit box. For example, they may have been in a wall safe behind a picture in the den or hidden under a mattress. However, all money and all intangibles, in fact all property, must be inventoried.

In the case of a single adult, the administrator must go to the home of the deceased and list all property found there. No firm guidelines exist to help the administrator choose what must be listed. The safest course of action is "when in doubt, include it in the inventory." A good approach is to take an inventory of each room, listing every item contained in that room. It is also a good idea to conduct this inventory with one or more reputable persons. Each of the witnesses should sign the inventory and note that it accurately reports all the items in the home.

If the deceased leaves a wife who will inherit almost everything in the estate, there is no need for a meticulous list of every item in the home. However, the administrator should specify all items of particular value such as oil paintings, valuable jewelry, antiques, books, and other articles of special monetary value. Other items can be listed in generalized groups, such as household furniture, $10,000.

The administrator should also inform the decedent's broker of the death since he must request a statement of the contents of the decedent's account. Many times, the decedent will have stocks or bonds listed in a street account. In other words, the brokerage house has the stock registered in its name. However, it is actually owned by the individual and is noted in any statement of his account. It is necessary to include this stock in the final inventory of the decedent's estate.

If the decedent's automobile is registered solely in his

name, it is best to get an immediate appraisal of the car for the inventory. It is also a good idea to check the insurance coverage to ascertain whether it will cover anyone who may be driving the car.

If the car is to be sold, it is best to sell it as soon as possible in view of the rapid depreciation of a car's value. However, it is important to remember that some states require court approval before an asset of the estate can be sold.

If the car has been left to a specified beneficiary, the administrator should seek to have the title transferred to that individual. Usually this can be done after the car has been appraised. The only time a transfer should not be effected promptly is when there is a possibility that the estate is insolvent, unable to pay its just debts, or when the terms of the will may be contested.

The administrator should gather all of the decedent's important papers. Such documents include homeowner's insurance policies, fire insurance abstracts, title insurance, deeds to real property, bank account books, passbooks, social security information, veterans' information, if applicable, and copyright or patent interests.

The administrator should also obtain several copies of the death certificate, either from the Department of Health and Vital Statistics, the County Clerk, or his state's equivalent of either of these departments. A death certificate should be attached to the notice which the administrator files with life insurance companies. This notice is the basis for claiming the face value of any life insurance policies held by the decedent.

Many individuals leave letters of instruction to the administrators. These documents are not legally binding, but they do apprise the administrator of additional ideas for the distribution of the estate. Therefore, a letter of instruction should be included with other important papers.

Most states require an administrator to complete his inventory and any necessary appraisals within sixty to ninety days of his official appointment by the probate court. The inventory and the appraisals must be filed within that period. By the time the administrator finishes this job, he may well find that the estate is worth much more than he originally thought and that these individual assets constitute a surprisingly large gross estate. However, while he is gathering this initial information, the administrator must be handling another important task: the management of the estate.

Managing the estate

The administrator is pledged to perform his tasks faithfully. Thus, the management of the estate between the date of death and the date of the actual distribution of the assets is an important and often demanding job. In addition to exercising sound judgment in day-to-day decisions, the administrator should establish and maintain good business records. When the administrator submits his final account to the probate court for its approval of final distribution, he must include a detailed record of all income received by the estate and all expenditures paid out by the estate. Thus, the importance of good record-keeping cannot be overemphasized. The lack of good record-keeping and the commingling of estate funds with personal funds are common errors of estate administrators.

To begin the bookkeeping, the administrator first opens a checking account in the name of the estate. This is an important safeguard since it prevents the administrator from accidentally mixing the funds of the estate with his personal funds. For example, the checking account might be opened in the following manner:

Estate of James Jones, deceased

by Robert Baker, (Administrator) (Executor). This should be done immediately. Thereafter, the administrator deposits all incoming money in this account. He also uses the checking account to pay all debts owed by the estate. One lawyer remarked that he even uses a check to pay for postage stamps. The emphasis placed on using this method is premised on the easy record which the check provides. A final accounting supported by attached checks covering each expenditure can protect the administrator from any charges of frittering away the "petty cash."

During the period from the date of death to the date of final distribution the estate receives income from various sources, including savings accounts, stocks, bonds, and real estate. In general, the estate must file an income tax return for that period. This is called a "Fiduciary Income Tax Return" and is filed on Federal Tax Form 1041. The administrator also applies to the local District Director of Internal Revenue for a tax identification number. This number is called an employer's identification number and is the same type of number required for partnerships and corporations. It is a simple process and is accomplished by writing the local office of the Internal Revenue for the application form SS4. Because of the extreme complexity in this area, it is recommended that an administrator consult his attorney, CPA, or the local Internal Revenue office for advice on specific problems.

The administrator is also required to file the decedent's income tax return for the period from the first of that year until the date of death. For example, if James Jones died on September 15th, a normal income tax return would be required for the income received from January 1 to September 15th of that year. Income received after death, such as dividends or interest are usually reported on the Fiduciary Income Tax Return Form 1041. The requirements for filing, paying, and receiving refunds are the same for decedents as for other taxpayers. The return is filed by the administrator who signs it in an appropriate descriptive manner to indicate his role (administrator of the deceased as well as the decedent on whose behalf he is acting). A joint return may be filed with the spouse of the deceased for the year of his death.

Most of the states have laws providing for the payment of an allowance to the surviving spouse or minor children during the period of the estate's administration. For example, Illinois statutes provide for the payment of a sum of money which is "reasonable for the support of such spouse and minor children for nine months after death of decedent in manner suited to such spouse's condition in life, taking into account the condition of the estate."

The various states provide for differing minimums and maximums of the dollar amount. The skillful administrator often works in conjunction with his attorney in petitioning the probate court for authorization to pay the surviving spouse and any minor children an adequate allowance. However, he must also take into account the condition of the estate. For example, if the assets of the estate are few, and the outstanding debts, both secured and unsecured, are large, the administrator may be forced to recommend a minimum allowance. On the other hand, if the estate is solvent, and the surviving spouse is in need of the funds, he may well recommend that the court authorize payment of the maximum allowance.

If the decedent had a going business, the administrator must secure proper authority to act for the decedent in furthering business interests. Illinois, for example, provides that an administrator may operate the decedent's business under the supervision of the court. This is the normal procedure if the business is a sole proprietorship. However, if the decedent belonged to a partnership, the surviving partner or partners are obligated to terminate the partnership's business. The partnership itself is dissolved unless there are provisions to the contrary in the partnership agreement.

Suppose the decedent owned stock in a corporation. In this case, the administrator may have one of two responsibilities. If the decedent was a moderate shareholder, the administrator's duties would be limited to a responsible supervision of the shares. However, the decedent may have been a majority stockholder. In that event, the administrator may have to take all necessary measures to continue the business. If the administrator is inexperienced in this area, he can consult his attorney, a reputable certified public accountant, and any trust officer with whom he has contact.

There are many other chores which the administrator

must perform while managing the estate. Subject to the restrictions of a particular state and the supervision of the court, he is allowed to buy and sell certain investments in stocks and bonds as his prudence dictates. He also is charged with collecting any rents from the decedent's real estate properties, as well as making any necessary repairs on the premises. If one tenant moves out, the administrator is empowered to negotiate a lease with a new tenant.

The administrator and the lawyer are entitled to a fee for administering and representing the estate. Most states have tables which provide for the computation of these fees. Usually, the fee is based on a percentage of the value of the estate. Once the fee is computed, the administrator petitions the probate court for its approval. Thereafter, the administrator provides for payment to himself and the lawyer. He then includes these amounts in his compilation of the estate tax return as well as in his final accounting to the probate court.

Perhaps the two most important rules of estate management are to use sound, prudent judgment when making decisions, and to establish an accurate bookkeeping system which fully accounts for every dollar paid into or out of the estate. Sound accounting practices also include the cardinal principle of keeping the estate's funds separate from personal funds of the administrator. If the administrator follows these general guides and seeks additional advice as the situation arises, he can rest assured that his final accounting of the estate will be approved by the probate court.

Determining claims, debts and paying taxes

Determination of claims. As was indicated, the administrator is required to submit a notice to creditors. Generally this notice must be published once a week for three consecutive weeks. It specifies a cutoff date by which all claims against the estate must be filed with the administrator or his attorney. According to most state laws, creditors must file their claims within six to nine months of the appointment of the administrator. If the administrator is satisfied that the submitted claim is valid, he is obligated to pay it out of the funds of the estate. If he is not satisfied that the claim is valid, he submits it to the court for a determination of its validity. If the estate's funds are limited, the administrator must determine the order in which he will pay the claims. Illinois laws, for example, state that funeral expenses are to be paid first, then awards to surviving spouse, then debts owed to the U.S. Government, then money owed to former employes, then expenses of the last illness, then any claim that the decedent held money in trust for a third party, then debts owed to the state government, and finally any other valid claim. The administrator must keep careful records of these payments since they will be required as part of the final accounting which he submits to the probate court.

Determine debts owed to decedent. After the publication of the death notice, the administrator must identify which accounts, if any, are owed to the decedent, and whether they are valid. If money is owed to the decedent, he must collect it. This means establishing a valid claim and then seeking payment from the debtor. If there is a question as to the validity of the debt or if the debtor refuses to pay, the administrator can go into court to get a determination of validity or to enforce the payment of the debt. Just as the administrator must accurately record all disbursements, so must he also record all money paid into the estate to satisfy debts owed to the decedent.

Payment of taxes. The administrator of an estate usually laments that there are just too many taxes to pay and too many returns with multiple and complex schedules to file. The income tax return of the decedent for the period from the start of the year to the date of his death, and the income tax return for the income of the estate within the period of administration are separate from the federal and state taxes on the value of the estate and any inheritances.

Usually the estate tax is imposed on the value of the estate at the time of the individual's death. However, if the administrator so decides, the tax can be levied on the value of the estate at an alternate valuation date one year after death. The Internal Revenue Code requires that an estate tax return be filed for the estate of every citizen or resident of the United States whose gross estate exceeds $60,000 in value at the date of death.

The return must be filed and the tax must be paid within nine months of the individual's death. However, an extension may be granted upon proper application by the administrator to the District Director of the Internal Revenue Service. If the decedent died testate, a certified copy of the will must be filed with the estate tax return. To many laymen, the estate tax return, Form 706, is the epitome of complexity. It consists of forty pages and includes nineteen schedules. These schedules require lists of the following items:

a. Real estate

b. Stocks and bonds

c. Mortgages, notes, and cash

d. Insurance

e. Jointly owned property

f. Other miscellaneous property

g. Transfers during decedent's life

h. Powers of appointment

i. Annuities

j. Funeral expenses and expenses incurred in administering property subject to claims

k. Debts of decedent and mortgages and liens

l. Net losses during administration and expenses incurred in administering property not subject to claims

m. Bequests to surviving spouse

n. Charitable gifts

o. Recapitulation (summary of schedules a. through n.)

p. Taxable estate—resident or citizen

q. Taxable estate—nonresident or not a citizen of the United States

r. Credit for tax on prior transfers

s. Credit for foreign death taxes

The names of these schedules correctly suggest that one cannot complete the return without a certain amount of knowledge and a great deal of patience. Although the instructions are extensive, few laymen attempt this task alone. Most rely on the professional help of a lawyer or certified public accountant.

In an estate tax return form, the items can be rounded off to whole-dollar amounts. Thus, any amount less than fifty cents is eliminated while any amount from fifty through ninety-nine cents is raised to the next highest dollar.

If the estate has more than one administrator, each must verify the return and sign it. These persons are responsible for the return and thus are fully liable to the government for any false returns.

Some states also impose a tax on the amount inherited by the beneficiary of a will. However, the inheritance tax return and payment are not technically a part of the administrator's duties. Since the different states vary on the aspects of this tax, it is necessary to check with an attorney, accountant, or the local probate court for the necessary information and forms.

Distributing the assets of an estate

At this point, the administrator's work is nearly done. His books list all income and expenditures. He has copies of the various tax returns. He has inventories and appraisals of all property owned by the decedent. He has paid all the valid claims submitted by creditors of the estate. He has collected any debts owed to the estate. He is now ready to distribute the assets to the respective beneficiaries of the will.

Initially, the administrator prepares a schedule for proposed distribution. If there is a will, the schedule lists the assets of the estate and the name of the beneficiary who is to receive them. If there is no will, the schedule lists the assets of the estate and the heirs named by the law for intestate succession. The probate court reviews the proposed schedule of distribution. If it fulfills the requirements, the court will issue an order approving the distribution of the estate.

After the schedule has been approved, the administrator actually distributes the assets. He should get receipts for each item from every beneficiary. These give the administrator a complete record of the disposition of all assets in the estate. Moreover, he will need to include these receipts in his final accounting to the probate court.

The receipts, by which the beneficiary acknowledges that he actually received the items, also protect the administrator from any possible charge of embezzlement or maladministration. As a further protection, however, the signing of the receipts should be witnessed by two or more disinterested persons.

RECEIPT OF BENEFICIARY OF ESTATE

Estate of James Jones, deceased
Probate Court No. 70–345

I hereby acknowledge receipt of the following described items from Robert Baker, administrator of the Estate of James Jones, deceased:

One (1) "Bristol Glass" antique vase, seven inches high, white with blue enameled flowers.

Twenty-five (25) Shares of American Telephone & Telegraph, common stock, Certificate No. 65T157-242.

$3,500, paid by check drawn on account of "Estate of James Jones, deceased," Check No. 321, National Bank of Anycity.

Signed and sealed this ____th day of __________ in the year 19_____.

____
(Name of Beneficiary)

Witnesses Date
____
____
____

Once the administrator has gathered all the receipts from the beneficiaries, he prepares his report to the court. This is known as the final accounting. The report includes records of all income and expenses, receipts for the distribution of the assets, and any other material required by the rules of the administrator's local probate court. If the probate court approves this accounting, it issues its order for a final discharge of the administrator. By this time, the administrator has come to appreciate the responsibility and the hard work involved in the "faithful performance" of his duties.

Chapter Thirteen

You and Your Lawyer

In the United States today there are over 300,000 lawyers, two-thirds in private practice. From these we select our personal legal counsellors.

It is unfortunate that most people procrastinate in choosing a lawyer until they are in serious trouble and need one in a hurry. Ideally, a lawyer should be considered in the same context as a family doctor or dentist. He should be thoroughly familiar with his client's history in order to do the best possible job in an emergency. At other times, the client may find that legal consultation will enable him to recognize possible legal difficulties more quickly than before. Being aware that there may be a legal problem enables the layman to know the consequences of signing a document or pursuing a given course of action. A good lawyer prevents hasty, legally unwise action from being taken. In sum, the presence of a family lawyer insures added security for the individual. He can be sure that advice is available and that the giver has a full understanding of his personal situation.

Before a lawyer is hired, his qualifications should be checked. The client should learn as much as he can about the lawyer's experience and reputation in the community. The lawyer's character and integrity should rank with those of the most respected men in the community.

In making his selection, an individual should consider his own personality as well as that of the potential lawyer. The ideal, of course, is to develop a professional, confidential relationship in which the client feels free to discuss any personal problem involving the law. Lawyers are bound by the canons of ethics to keep in confidence anything a client says during an attorney-client conversation. Therefore, it is important for the client to choose an attorney with impeccable credentials.

In case of special legal problems, such as complex trusts, the layman should seek out a specialist in wills and estates. It stands to reason that one who devotes his time exclusively to wills and estates will be able to solve the client's problems more quickly and competently than one who devotes only about a quarter of his time to that particular area. Complex and intricate tax questions, particularly if they concern small businesses and corporations, need the special expertise of a knowledgeable tax lawyer. And while legal advice can be very costly, in many instances a good lawyer can save his client money. It is best, of course, to discuss the subject of fees before any work is done, so there will be no disagreements later.

A high-quality lawyer's reputation is built on sound legal work. Satisfied clients usually will recommend their attorneys. Another reliable source of referrals is the bank. An officer of a bank may hesitate to make only one recommendation; but, more than likely, he would be quite happy to suggest four or five qualified people and let you, as the potential client, make the final decision. Many communities also provide some guidance in locating legal services. For little or no fee, a client can be referred to a lawyer who is equipped to handle his special problem. Finally, if a client is moving to a new community, he might ask his present lawyer to recommend a competent attorney there.

Many times, people simply cannot afford legal advice. An increasing number of communities have established

Neighborhood Legal Aid Services to handle cases without a fee. Potential clients are first interviewed to determine whether their inability to pay fits within national guidelines. If so, their legal problems are handled without charge. If the interview determines that the individual can afford his own attorney, he is given the names of several lawyers who might handle the case for a small fee. Of course, in all but minor criminal cases, the individual is always entitled to a free lawyer. Sometimes this will be provided by a public defender's office. In other areas free legal help is dispensed through court-appointed lawyers. The judge usually has a list of local attorneys and makes his appointments on a rotation basis.

Once a lawyer has been selected, the layman should attempt to do his part to maintain a good lawyer-client relationship. A good association will achieve better results and will mean more efficiency for the attorney and more legal advice at less cost to the client.

The first prerequisite for a good relationship is that the client be open, honest, and thorough in describing his situation. Too often, a client leaves out little, but important, facts because he wants to convince his lawyer that he was "in the right." Later, the lawyer will discover the true facts. The result: at best, needless work will be expended; at worst, an amicable solution may be jeopardized because the parties and attorneys were acting under a misapprehension of the true facts. A lawyer must have all the available facts at his disposal in order to give the best possible advice.

A second suggestion is to refrain from telling the attorney how to proceed. Certainly, the client must make any final decisions about whether to sue, whether to accept a proposed settlement, or whether to sign a contract. But he should make an effort not to interfere with his lawyer's handling of the case. In addition to wasting time, it might jeopardize the attorney-client relationship. The methods of legal procedures are the tools of the lawyer's trade which he acquired through long hours of study and practice. Permitting him to proceed with no interference will enable him to gather the best possible information and consult the best resources in order to advise the client of the relative merits of possible courses of action. Based upon this information, the client can make his own final decision on the matter.

Another point is to use the advice you purchased. A frequent complaint of lawyers is that if they tell the client what he wants to hear, the client is happy and follows his preconceived course. However, when a recommendation is contrary to what he wants to do, the client may ignore the advice of his attorney.

Finally, be sure to discuss the matter of fees with your attorney. Too many people are so afraid of high fees that they do not talk about them until after the case. It is best to discuss the amount of the fee with the attorney *before* any legal advice is rendered. A full and honest discussion at this time will prevent needless disagreements and hard feelings later. Law is like any other service and fees are a necessary part of it. In most areas, courts or local bar associations have established schedules of suggested minimum fees for different legal services, and lawyers often voluntarily follow these schedules. Schedules are based on the following factors:

- The time and labor required
- The novelty of the question
- The customary fee for similar legal services
- The amount of money involved and the results obtained
- The experience and reputation of the lawyer performing the services
- Whether or not the client is a regular one

These are all factors to keep in mind in order to establish and maintain a good lawyer-client relationship. Following these guidelines should help produce good legal advice and a satisfied client.

A final word of advice may be given on the nature of the lawyer. He has been trained to serve you, and his competence lies in his special abilities to understand and use the special *language* of the law. He has been trained to come to grips with the legal questions you may have by his familiarity not only with the laws of the land but also with cases similar to your own. Too often, after the tangle of 300 years of legislation, the precedents and regulations applying to a specific case are incomprehensible to all the experts in this field. But the client should never feel in awe of this special expertise. While more lawyers than members of any other profession have become president of the United States, many lawyers have also landed in jail. And, in the end, the quality of the legal service you receive rests in large part on the judgment you exercise in selecting someone with competence and integrity to represent your interests.

The rules prohibiting lawyers from advertising their services or soliciting cases have gone a long way toward establishing and maintaining the concept of the law as a profession noted for its high quality and ethics. It is the lawyer's ability to give sound legal advice which establishes his reputation, and, in the end, this is his promise of professional success and your guarantee of satisfactory legal counsel.

Glossary

Abatement (reduction or decrease): the proportionate reduction of a claim when the fund used for payment is insufficient to meet the full amount of the claim. Also, the termination of a lawsuit due, for instance, to the death of a party.

Ab initio (Latin, "from the beginning"): a transaction or document from its inception. For example, an insurance policy may be held to be invalid *ab initio* or from the purported issuance of the policy.

Abstract of title: a summary of deeds and other documents comprising the history of a title to land.

Accord and satisfaction: an agreement between two or more persons which settles a disputed claim or lawsuit through the payment of some amount or the performance of some action in satisfaction of the asserted claim.

Acquittal: a release from an obligation when used in reference to contracts. In criminal law, a person is acquitted if the charge against him is dismissed either through a verdict of acquittal or by some formal and conclusive legal procedure.

Action (also called a suit): a proceeding in a court of law by which one party sues another to secure the enforcement or protection of a right or the redress of a wrong. Civil actions concern private rights and injuries. A criminal action is taken to redress a public wrong.

Ademption: a cancellation of a legacy. It occurs when an action of the testator is interpreted as an intentional revocation of the legacy.

Adjudication: normally the pronouncement of the judgment or decree in a court case. In bankruptcy proceedings, it refers to the court order declaring that the debtor is bankrupt.

Administrative law: a branch of law governing procedure before various government agencies of the executive and legislative branch.

Administrator: the person appointed by a court to settle an estate, usually when there is no will. When it is a woman, the word "administratrix" is used.

Adverse possession: a means of acquiring title to property through occupancy for a specified number of years.

Affidavit: a written and sworn statement witnessed by a notary public or another official possessing the authority to administer oaths.

A mensa et thoro: a divorce by which the parties are legally separated. It is distinct from a divorce *a vinculo* which completely dissolves or breaks the bonds of matrimony.

Amicus curiae (Latin, "a friend of the court"): a person who has no legal right to appear before the court in a certain proceeding. However, the court allows him to introduce evidence, argument, or authority because he has a collateral interest in the case.

Annual percentage rate: a term required to be disclosed on all credit transactions under the Truth in Lending Law; it describes the cost, in percentage, of having credit.

Annulment: formal invalidation of a marriage by means of a court decree declaring that a marriage is a nullity from the beginning.

Arraignment: the process of advising an accused person of the criminal charge against him and allowing him to state his answer to the charge. This proceeding takes place in a court.

Arrest: a legally authorized act by which a person is deprived of his liberty.

Arrest of judgment: the act of postponing a judgment.

Articles of agreement: a written statement comprising the terms of an agreement.

Assignment: the legal transfer of a claim, a right, or an interest in property to another person.

Attachment: the seizure of persons or property by means of a legal writ, summons, or another judicial order.

Attestation of a will: the act of subscribing one's name as a witness to the execution of a will.

Attorney-at-law: an officer of the court and a member of the bar. He is empowered to give legal advice and to conduct legal proceedings on behalf of others.

Attorney-in-fact: a person who is authorized by another to act in the latter's behalf. An attorney-in-fact is not necessarily a member of the bar.

Averment: a statement of facts in a legal pleading.

Bailee: the legal term for a person to whom property is entrusted. It has no relation to criminal bail.

Bailment: the temporary transfer of personal property by one person in trust to another. The property is delivered for a special purpose with the understanding that it will be returned when the purpose of the bailment is carried out.

Bearer paper: a negotiable instrument which can be transferred by delivery. It does not require endorsement.

Bench warrant: a process issued by the court for the arrest of a person guilty of contempt or indicted for a crime.

Beneficiary: the person named in a will or trust to receive property.

Bequeath: the legal word which refers to the giving of personal property by will.

Bill of costs: an itemized statement of authorized allowances and expenses that can be charged to the unsuccessful party to a lawsuit.

Bill of indictment (or indictment): a written legal document that accuses a person of a crime.

Bill of particulars: a document listing the details of a claim for which a suit is brought.

Bill of sale: a written statement by which one person transfers to another his rights to personal property.

Bona fide: a Latin phrase meaning that one acts "in good faith," without intention to defraud or deceive.

Bond: a formal certificate of a debt; also defined as an interest-bearing certificate of a public or private debt.

Burden of proof: the duty of a party in a civil lawsuit to present sufficient proof to establish a disputed fact.

Calendar (or trial list): the list of cases to be tried during a court term.

Capacity: the ability recognized by law to take legal action.

Capias (Latin): a class of writs that authorize a court officer to take a defendant into custody or, in other words, to arrest him.

Carrier: commonly, one who is hired to transport persons or property.

Case law: a branch of law consisting of court decisions. It is distinct from statutes and other sources of law.

Causa mortis: a Latin phrase meaning "in contemplation of death," usually applied in connection with gifts made shortly before the donor's death.

Cause of action: the legal basis for a lawsuit by one person against another.

Caveat emptor: a Latin phrase meaning "let the buyer beware."

Caveat venditor: a Latin phrase meaning "let the seller beware."

Certiorari (Latin, "to be made certain"): a legal proceeding by which a court reviews the decision of a lower court or governmental agency.

Cestui qui trust (Latin): the 'beneficiary of a trust."

Challenge: the party's right to object to a juror during the selection of the jury for a trial.

Charge: an accusation that a person has committed a crime. In a jury trial, the charge constitutes instructions on law given by the judge to the jury at the end of the trial.

Chattel: an item of personal property as distinguished from real estate.

Citation: an order directing a person to appear in a legal proceeding.

Clerk of court: an officer in charge of the records and proceedings of a court.

Codicil: a document, executed with all the formality of a will, used to amend the provisions of an existing will.

Comity of states: the practice by which the courts of one state recognize the laws and judicial decisions of another state.

Commutation: a change from a greater to a lesser punishment in criminal law.

Complaint (also called a "petition" or "declaration"): the legal statement of the plaintiff's claim of grievance. It identifies both plaintiff and defendant and usually gives the residence of the parties, the alleged basis for the defendant's legal liability, and a request for damages or another remedy.

Condemnation: the appropriation of private property for public use. Compensation is required.

Construction: the process of determining the true meaning of a legal document, such as a "contract" or a "will."

Contempt: the disobedience of the rules, orders, and procedures of a court or a legislative body.

Conveyance: a transfer of a right to property; usually an interest in real property.

Corpus delicti (Latin, "body of a crime"): the necessary substantial evidence or proof that a crime has been committed.

Credit: the sale of property or services in exchange for a promise of deferred payment.

Creditor: a person to whom a debt is owing.

Damages: Compensation recovered through the court by an individual who has sustained injury to his person, property, or rights because of an illegal act of another.

Decree: a final judgment or determination of a court.

Deed: a written document signed by the owner of real estate which transfers ownership to another person.

De facto: a Latin phrase meaning "in fact," usually used to describe a situation which exists in fact, irrespective of any design or operation of law.

Default: the failure of a party to a legal proceeding to perform an act required by law, as in the failure to appear and defend a lawsuit.

De jure: a Latin phrase meaning "in accordance with law." For example, a corporation may have a valid charter and may be acting within its powers. It is, therefore, a *de jure* corporation.

Demurrer: a pleading by one party to a legal action that admits the truth of the matter alleged by the other party but declares it is insufficient in law to sustain the claim.

Deponent: a person who makes a written statement under oath.

Deposition: the written testimony of a witness. It is transcribed according to law while the person is under oath but not in open court.

Descent: the inheritance of real property when the owner dies without a will.

Devisee: a person who is given real property under a will.

Disability: the absence of legal capability to carry out an act.

Distribution: the allocation and delivery of a decedent's property to his heirs or those named in a will.

Due process of law: the required procedures for depriving someone of life, liberty, or property through governmental action. These procedures are guaranteed by the U.S. Constitution.

Easement: the right of the owner of one piece of real estate to use the land of his neighbor for a special purpose.

Ejectment: the legal remedy available to a landowner for recovery of real estate from persons who have no right to be on it.

Eminent domain: the power of the state to appropriate private property for public use.

Enjoin: to require a person by a writ of injunction to perform or to desist from an act.

Escheat: an old English term used to describe the right of the state to take property when there are no heirs surviving the owner.

Estate: all property, real or personal, tangible or intangible, in which a person has an interest, usually referring to the total a person has at his death.

Et al.: a Latin phrase meaning "and others."

Et ux.: a Latin phrase meaning "and wife."

Exception: a legal term for a formal objection to the action or ruling of the court during a trial.

Executor: the person named in a will to carry out its terms. When it is a woman, the word "executrix" is used.

Ex parte: a Latin phrase meaning "on one side only." Usually, it describes a proceeding in which only one side has made application and only one side is heard.

Family car doctrine: a doctrine by which the head of the household is liable for injuries caused by the negligence of other members of his household while operating the family car. Not all states accept this doctrine.

Felony: a serious crime, usually punishable by imprisonment or death, as distinct from a minor crime or misdemeanor.

Fiduciary: a person holding property in a trust capacity for the benefit of another. Executors, guardians, and trustees are fiduciaries.

Finance charge: a term required to be disclosed on all credit transactions under the Truth in Lending Law; it describes the total of all costs which the consumer must pay for obtaining credit.

Garnishment: a procedure through which a debtor's property is attached by a creditor while it is in the hands of a third person, such as the debtor's employer.

Grand jury: a body of local citizens who hear an *ex parte* presentation of evidence by a prosecuting attorney and who must then determine whether the evidence is sufficient to indict, or officially charge, the suspect with a specific crime.

Habeas corpus: a Latin phrase meaning "have the body." It describes a proceeding by which a writ is issued to someone having custody of a person, ordering him to bring the prisoner to court to determine if he is being unlawfully detained.

Holographic will: a will written, signed, and dated by the testator in his own handwriting.

Indemnity: an agreement by which one person promises to protect or to reimburse another for loss or damages.

Information: a written document charging a person with a criminal offense without the intervention of a grand jury.

Inquest: a judicial inquiry.

Joint tenancy: joint tenants who own an equal interest in the same property, all of which passes to the survivor.

Judgment: the official decision of a court.

Judgment creditor: the party in a lawsuit who has won a money judgment against his debtor.

Judgment debtor: a person who owes the money judgment.

Judgment lien: a lien binding the property, usually real estate, of a judgment debtor.

Judicial notice: the doctrine by which the court accepts certain matter without demanding evidence. Such matter include state laws, historical events, geographical data, etc.

Jurisdiction: the legal authority of a court to hear a case or conduct other proceedings.

Justice of the peace: a judicial officer having jurisdiction of a limited nature over minor cases, both civil and criminal.

Legacy: a provision in a will which leaves certain personal property to a named individual. It is also known as a bequest.

Legatee: a person who is given personal property under a will.

Letters of administration: documents usually issued by a probate court giving an administrator the authority to administer the estate of the deceased person.

Letters of guardianship: a court document that serves as a guardian's authority to act.

Letters testamentary: documents issued by a probate court giving a person named as executor in a will the authority to administer the estate of the person who made the will.

Levy: the seizure and sale of property by the court to satisfy a garnishment or judgment.

Lien: a claim against property.

Life estate: a lifetime interest in property. This interest terminates upon the death of the individual.

Life tenant: a person who holds a lifetime interest in property.

Lis pendens (Latin, "pending suit"): a notice advising those interested to examine the pending legal action.

Malfeasance: performance of a wrongful act.

Misdemeanor: an act that violates public law. It is usually punishable by a fine or a short term of imprisonment.

Misfeasance: the improper performance of a lawful act.

Mistrial: a court proceeding that is terminated because of a procedural error.

Nolo contendere (Latin, "I will not contest"): a plea similar to a plea of guilty; used only in a criminal action.

Notary public: a public official whose duty is to administer oaths and witness numerous types of official documents.

Novation: a new debt, contract, or obligation that supersedes one previously made.

Nuisance: a tort arising from a person's use of his property; generally when he causes annoyance, damage, or danger to others by such use.

Nuncupative will: an oral will by which a person disposes of his property in the event of his death. In many states, this type of will has been ruled invalid by state statute.

Option (in contract law): a privilege extended to one person giving him the opportunity to purchase another's property at a specified price within a designated time limit.

Order: a written direction of a court or a judge, other than a judgment.

Per capita (Latin, "by the head"): a method of dividing property left by a decedent. The property is distributed among the number of individuals equally related to the decedent so that each receives an equal share.

Per stirpes (Latin, "by the root"): a class or group takes and divides amongst themselves the share their ancestor, such as a parent, would have received.

Petit jury: a body of local citizens, usually twelve, who are chosen to hear and decide the verdict in civil and criminal cases.

Plea (or answer): a document filed by the defendant to contest the claim of the plaintiff. It admits or denies the various claims set forth in the complaint.

Pleading: the process by which parties to a civil lawsuit present written statements of their respective contentions.

Pledge: the transfer of title or possession of personal property to a creditor as security for a debt.

Probate: the judicial procedure to determine that a certain document claimed to be a will of the decedent is in fact valid and properly executed and to supervise administration and distribution of the estate.

Proximate cause: that which in the ordinary course of events, unbroken by another cause, produces an injury and without which the injury would not have taken place.

Quitclaim deed: a document by which a person transfers all of his interest in a piece of real estate. It does not include a warranty of title, nor does it profess that the title is valid.

Remand: to recommit a case to a lower court for corrective action.

Replevin: a legal action instituted to recover possession of property that was unlawfully taken or detained.

Replication (or reply): a pleading filed by the plaintiff to answer the material set forth in the defendant's plea.

Residuary estate: the portion of a decedent's estate that is left after the payment of specific legacies, debts, and estate administration expenses.

Revocation of a will: an act by a person who has made a will indicating his intention that the will shall no longer be effective.

Rule: a standard or regulation to govern judicial and other procedures.

Satisfaction of judgment: a document stating that a recorded judgment has been paid.

Seisin: the ownership or the right to immediate possession of land or an interest in real estate.

Statute: a law passed by a legislative body.

Statute of frauds: a series of legal provisions requiring certain contracts to be in writing.

Statute of limitations: a law prescribing that a suit on certain types of claims must be brought within a specific time period.

Substantive law: the branch of law that prescribes legal rights.

Summons: a written document notifying the defendant that an action has been started against him and requiring him to appear in court within a specified length of time to answer to the complaint.

Surrogate: the title sometimes given to the judge who presides in the court where estates of decedents are administered.

Testator: the person making the will. When it is a woman, the word "testatrix" is used.

Title: evidence of a person's right to the ownership of property.

Tort: a wrong, other than a breach of contract, committed upon the person or property of another.

Trust: the holding of property by one person for the benefit of another.

Usury: a term describing the imposition of an illegal rate of interest.

Venireman: a member of a panel of jurors.

Venue: the place where a legal proceeding takes place.

Verdict: a judge or jury's decision on a matter submitted to them in trial.

Verification: an affidavit or statement under oath confirming the contents of a document.

Waiver: the act of intentionally abandoning a right, claim, or privilege.

Writ: a court order requiring a public official to perform a specified act.

Index